EIGHTEEN SONG CYCLES

LOTTE LEHMANN

Eighteen
Song Cycles

STUDIES IN THEIR INTERPRETATION

WITH A FOREWORD BY
NEVILLE CARDUS

CASSELL · LONDON

CASSELL & COMPANY LTD
35 Red Lion Square, London WC1
Sydney, Toronto
Johannesburg, Auckland

First published 1971

I.S.B.N. 0 304 93842 4

Printed in Great Britain by
The Camelot Press Ltd, London and Southampton
F. 771

I dedicate this book to the memory of Paul Ulanowsky who for many years was my devoted accompanist and with whom I realized complete harmony and understanding.

ACKNOWLEDGEMENTS

I would like to thank my good friend, Sir Neville Cardus, for writing the Foreword to this book, which will gain dignity and added value by his contribution. I am also most grateful to him for introducing me to my publisher, Mr David Ascoli, to whom goes my gratitude for the care which he has devoted to editing the manuscript and improving my sometimes questionable English.

My sincere thanks to my friend Frances Holden for her constant encouragement and for allowing me access to her marvellous library.

Last but not least, I must thank Margaret Hoenig who not only retyped my manuscript but who also helped me with valuable suggestions.

CONTENTS

FOREWORD
by NEVILLE CARDUS

In opera Lotte Lehmann was not so much a singer who could act but, rather, a great protean actress who could sing with a voice richly engaging the ear and, by its range of colour and inflection, arresting to the sense of theatre and to the histrionic imagination. In the beginning was, for Lehmann, the word, the deed, the scene, the personal presence. She was not an opera singer who, for various parts, disguised herself externally as Sieglinde, Leonore, the Marschallin and the rest; she identified herself with each part, became as though transfused, blood and mind, into the part. She was not just a 'character' actress, drawing a blank cheque on our preconceptions. Her range was wide; she personified Sophie, Oktavian and the Marschallin over the years in *Der Rosenkavalier*. She was Rosalinde in *Die Fledermaus* to the vivacious essence of Rosalinde; she was Leonore in *Fidelio*, living image of 'das ewig-Weibliche'. She ranged through the entire gamut of emotion.

As she came on the darkened stage at the beginning of Act 1 of *Die Walküre*, and saw the exhausted Siegmund lying prone, and whispered: 'Ein fremder Mann', we could almost hear the heart of Sieglinde beating. She leaned forward, the whole woman of her expressing curiosity, apprehension and—also— an intuitive, prophetic sympathy, an unaware sister-love. I recall with vivid return of reality her marvellous moment when Sieglinde says: 'Hush! Let me listen to thy voice. I heard it as a child'—('O, still! Lass mich der Stimme lauschen; mich dünkt, ihren Klang hört' ich als Kind'). The voice of Lehmann passed almost into silence as she sang 'hört' ich als Kind'; we could feel her mind going back in time and listening within itself for long-forgotten tendernesses. Then Lehmann gave a quick gasp of ecstasy, and her 'doch nein!' caught at our heartstrings.

As the Dyer's Wife in *Die Frau ohne Schatten* of Strauss, she mingled a poignant sympathy with her conception of the woman's discontent and sexual self-flagellation. As the Marschallin she was all tight-lipped resignation as she pronounced the word 'Vorbei!' As the Marschallin, in Act I, she was a young girl again, laughing capriciously when the unexpected intruder is not the Feldmarschall, her husband, but merely a visitor. 'Es ist ein Besuch!' The waltz phrases in the music became incarnate in Lehmann; the whole woman of her danced.

At a rehearsal of *Fidelio* Toscanini found himself transfixed by Lehmann, and he temporarily, for a split minute, forgot his sway over the orchestra, and everybody else. He actually relaxed his baton and cried out to Lehmann: 'You are an artist!' It was not Toscanini's custom to bandy words and compliments with opera singers.

She was the artist whose style was the woman herself, a richly natured woman, sensitive and fine-minded and civilized. She is still Lehmann, the fully realized woman, stored with experience, afflicted by physical pain, philosophical and endowed with healing humour. Herself, she is a gifted writer of poetry, and a painter. What is bred in the bone comes out even in an opera singer. Her love of words was a potent factor of her artistic appeal, as I have already hinted. The imperishable stuff of Lehmann is preserved in one of her verses:

> So hört' ich wieder deiner Stimme Ton,
> Die einst mein Herz erzittern machte . . .
> Ich lachte
> Ob der versunknen Illusion.
> Wie seltsam: ich versteh'es kaum
> Dass dieser schien der einzig Eine . . .
> und doch: ich weine
> Um einen toten Traum.

> *And I heard again the sound of your voice*
> *which once made my heart tremble . . .*
> *I laughed*
> *at the lost illusion.*
> *How strange: I can scarce realize*

that he seemed to me the only one . . .
And yet, I weep
over a dead dream.

As a Lieder singer she did not consistently satisfy the purists. She enlarged the canvas. Her interpretation of 'Erlkönig' rendered as much homage to Goethe as to Schubert. Myself, I had the same embracing experiences at a Lehmann Lieder recital as at her opera reincarnations. In this book she bestows on us her harvestings—enriching, I think, not only to students of Lieder but to the oldest of music lovers. It is wise, wiser maybe than she knows. It teaches to the purist, insists on the individuality of the learner. But, more rewarding still, it is a book which reflects and sustains our impressions, our devotion to and admiration of, Lotte Lehmann. Anyhow, I speak for myself.

NEVILLE CARDUS

London
June, 1971

INTRODUCTION

Interpretation means: individual understanding and reproduction. How then is it possible to teach interpretation? It seems almost paradoxical to emphasize the necessity for individuality in interpretation and at the same time want to explain my own conceptions of singing. First and foremost I want to say that this book will fail in its purpose, if the young singers, for whom I am writing it, should consider my conceptions as something final and try to imitate them instead of developing their own interpretations which should spring with originality and vitality from within themselves.

For imitation is, and can only be, the enemy of artistry. Everything which has the breath of life is changeable: a momentary feeling often makes me alter an interpretation. Do not build up your songs as if they were encased in stone walls. They must soar from the warm, pulsing beat of your own heart, blessed by the interpretation of the moment. Only from life itself may life be born.

What I want to try to explain here is not any final interpretation, but an approach which may be an aid towards the development of your individual conceptions. I want to point a way which might lead from the lack of understanding of those singers, who seem to consider only voice quality and smooth technique, to the boundless world of expression. And it will be seen that there is not just *one*, but an infinitely varied pattern of ways, which lead to this goal. Only he who seeks it with his whole heart will find his own approach to interpretation.

I have listened to many young singers, and have found with ever increasing astonishment that they consider their preparation finished when they have developed a lovely voice, a serviceable technique and musical accuracy. At this point they consider themselves ready to appear before the public.

Certainly no one can question that technique is the all-important foundation—the a b c of singing. It goes without saying that no one can master *too* carefully the technique of voice production. Complete mastery of the voice as an instrument is an ideal towards which every singer must work assiduously. But that technique must be mastered to the point of being *unconscious*, before you can really become an *interpreter*.

That God-given instrument—the voice—must be capable of responding with the greatest subtley to every shade of every emotion. But it must be subordinate, it must only be the foundation, the soil from which true art flowers.

It is only with the greatest hesitation that I dare put into words my ideas regarding the interpretation of Lieder and of French Chansons. For is it not dangerous to give definite expression to something which must essentially be born from inspiration and be, above all things, vitally alive? Yet I have so often been urged by experienced musicians to help the younger generation with such a book as this, that I have decided to put down my ideas in spite of my hesitation. But I should like to take as the motto of this book Goethe's words from Faust: 'Grau, teurer Freund, ist alle Theorie—und grün des Lebens gold'ner Baum.' ('Grey, dear friend, is all theory and green the golden tree of life'.) So may you young, aspiring singers, for whom I write this book, take the fullness of my experience, of my studies, of my development and discoveries as the simile of the golden tree, but it is for you to pluck the fresh, living fruit from its branches. It is for you to infuse with your own spirit, that which comes to you as advice, as suggestion. When you have a deep inner conviction about a song— the words as well as the music—then be sure that your conception is a right one, even though it may differ from what is traditional.

For what is tradition?

The mother earth, from which springs everything which may grow and flower. The creator's conception of an idea, a work of art, which has been handed down from generation to generation, which has been cherished and developed until it spreads before us as a network of determined paths which are to be followed without questioning. Strict tradition dictates that not a single step may be taken from these paths.

But you are young and the youth of every generation is eager and should be eager for new ways. You have a different viewpoint from that of your parents and teachers. You do not necessarily care for the old, recommended, well-travelled roads. You want to venture into new, alluring fields, to lose yourselves in the mysterious depths of the forests. I know that I am committing a fearful sin against holy tradition when I say: Excellent! Seek your own way! Do not become paralysed and enslaved by the set patterns which have been created of old. Build from your own youthful feeling, your own hesitant thoughts and your own flowering perception—and help to further that beauty which has grown from the roots of tradition. Do not misunderstand me: naturally I do not mean that you should despise the aspirations and the knowledge of earlier generations. I only mean that tradition is not an *end* but a *beginning*. Do not lose yourself in its established pattern but let your own conceptions and expression be nourished from it as a flower blooms from the life forces provided by its roots. Simply let them bloom more richly in the light of your own imagination. Certainly you will make mistakes. You will often take the wrong road before you find your true way, just as I have. I grew up in Germany, in the tradition of Lieder singing. I might have come much earlier to that holiest of all—the Lied, had I not been so completely immersed in the theatre. I lived, so to speak, in the opera house and took my few concerts on the side without much preparation. May Schubert, Schumann, Brahms and Wolf forgive me for the sins which I committed in their name!

As the reputation which I had won through my work in opera became known in other countries, concerts became more frequent, so that there dawned upon me a new and overpowering realization: that as a Lieder singer, I was at the very dawn of an awakening.

This was the first step: the awareness of my ignorance.

My approach was a hesitant one and I often went astray. In the beginning I felt that this came more from the words than from the music. If I had not been born a singer, endowed with a touch of the golden quality of voice of my good mother, I would without doubt have become an actress. Actually, throughout my whole life I have envied those who are free to

B

3

express without the limitation of opera singing. So in singing Lieder, the words, the poem became the main thing for me, until—much later—I found and captured the true balance between words and music.

In general I find that the words are too much neglected. On the other hand I should like to protect you from the stage which I had to go through: of feeling first the *word* and only finally the *melody*. Learn to feel *as a whole* that which *is* a whole in complete harmony: poem *and* music. Neither can be more important than the other. First there was the poem. That gave the inspiration for the song. Like a frame, music encloses the word picture—and now comes your interpretation, breathing life into this work of art, welding words and music with equal feeling into one whole, so that the poet sings and the composer becomes poet and two arts are born anew as one.

That is the Lied.

Dynamic shadowings are like sketches but the enchanting in-between colours alone can give the tone picture a personal quality. There is a clear, silvery *pianissimo* which sounds light and ethereal, and there is a veiled *pianissimo* which trembles with passion and restrained desire. There is a bright *forte*— strong and forceful like a fanfare—and a darkly coloured *forte*, which breaks out sombrely, in grief and pain. The 'veiled' *piano* which I have mentioned is a vibration of tone which has no place in the realm of technique and yet, in my opinion, it cannot be neglected in inspired singing; in fact, it is of the utmost importance. How much restrained passion can be conveyed by a veiled tone and how much floating purity in a clear flute-like *pianissimo*!

One seldom hears a voice which is capable of altering its timbre. For me it goes absolutely against the grain to sing always with the same tone colour. Dynamic gradations seem dead without the animating interplay of dark and light, clear and restrained.

It almost seems superfluous to emphasize that a phrase must always have a main word and, with it, a musical highpoint. Yet it is incredible how often this elementary and self-evident fact is neglected. Again and again I am astonished by a lack of musical feeling for the essential nature of a phrase. Every phrase must be sung with a sweeping line, not just as a series of words which have equal weight and no grace. It is the floating sweep, not just a long breath, which makes the beautifully rounded phrase. The best help in learning to feel how a phrase should sound is to *recite the poem*. In speaking, you would never give equal emphasis to every syllable as you so often do in singing—through eagerness to hold the tempo or to give each note its exact value or above all to show that your singing is supported by excellent breath control. In my opinion, more important than all these factors, valuable as they are, is giving life to the phrase through emphasizing what is important and making subsidiary the words which have only a connecting value.

Singing should never follow a straight line. It should have a sweeping flow, it should glide in soft rhythmical waves which follow one another harmoniously. (I am referring here to the musical line of a *phrase* and not to sliding from syllable to syllable which generally has a sentimentalizing effect and should only be made use of most sparingly.) Each new sentence should have a new beginning, the new thought should live, should breathe, emerging from the previous sentence. Create yourself each new thought as if it had just come to life in you. Let it arise from your own inner feeling. Do not sing just a melody, sing a *poem*. Music lifting the poem from the coldness of the spoken word has transfigured it with new beauty. But you, the singer, must make your listeners realize that the poem, far from losing its beauty through becoming music, has been ennobled, born anew in greater splendour and loveliness. Never forget: recite the poem when you sing—sing the music as you recite the words of the poem in the Lied. Only from the equal value of both creations can perfection arise.

I should like to touch here upon a question, which often arises, as to whether a woman should sing Lieder which, according to the poem, are written for a man. I say with emphasis: Yes!

Why should a singer be denied a vast number of wonderful songs, if she has the power to create an illusion which will make her audience believe in it? It would be a very sad indication of incapacity if one could not awaken in the listener sufficient imagination to carry him with one into the realms of creative fantasy. If you sing of love and happiness, you must be a young person convincingly—and perhaps in reality you are neither young nor beautiful. The stage sets limitations which simply do not exist on the concert platform: on the stage you *see* the person who is represented, your representation must in some measure correspond outwardly to the character which you portray. The imagination of the audience has its limits: it sees the figure before it in the framework of the role, surrounded by the characters of the story which is being unfolded. In a certain sense it is very much more difficult to retain the illusion of a portrayal when the limits are set by reality. On the other hand on the concert stage it is the unlimited power of your art which must change you into just that figure which you seek to bring to life. You are without any material aids, without any gestures, without the footlights which separate so wonderfully the world of the stage from the world of reality. You stand close to the audience. Almost one with it, you take it, so to speak, by the hand and say: 'Let us live this song together! Forget with me that I cannot have a thousand real forms, for I will make you believe in all these forms as I change my personality in every song. Let us together put aside reality, and let us, singing and hearing, soar away into the limitless realms of fantasy.' As Mignon says in Goethe's *Wilhelm Meister*—'und jene himmlischen Gestalten, sie fragen nicht nach Mann und Weib . . .' ('And there each celestial presence shall question naught of man and maid . . .')—so the singer soars above all limitations, is young, is beautiful, is man or woman, longing and fulfillment, death and resurrection.

It is my hope that through this book I may open a door which may lead you to feeling what you understand—and understanding what you feel.

The road to the ever unattainable goal, perfection, is long and hazardous. No success with the public, no criticisms however wonderful, could ever make me believe that I have reached 'perfection.' Everyone has his own limitations and imperfections. Everyone is to a certain extent the victim of his nerves, his momentary mood and disposition. I am rightly reproached for breathing too often and so breaking phrases. This is one of my unconquerable nervous inadequacies. It is often not enough to *know* and to *feel* and to *recognize*. Human, all too human are the weaknesses under which all of us suffer,

6

each in our own way. In a certain sense, it seems that perfect technique and interpretation which comes from the heart and soul can never go hand in hand and that this combination is an unattainable ideal. For the very emotion which enables the singer to carry her audience with her into the realm of artistic experience is the worst enemy of a crystal-clear technique. Perhaps, in this case, I am the well-known fox for whom the grapes hang too high! But I have found, again and again, that a singer who delights in technique (much as I may admire her virtuosity) still, in some way, leaves my heart cold. Do not misunderstand me: control of the voice is the soil from which interpretation springs. But do not despair over small imperfections, over mistakes which are difficult to eliminate. For if your spirit can soar above technique and float in the lofty regions of creative art, you have fulfilled your mission as a singer. For what mission can be greater than that of giving to the world hours of exaltation in which it may forget the misery of the present, the cares of everyday life, and lose itself in the eternally pure world of harmony?

THE SONG CYCLE

The interpretation of a cycle is, it seems to me, the ideal form of Lieder singing. Without the interruptions of applause one can, with complete inner absorption, maintain the tension which encloses a long series of songs. And even if the songs are absolutely different in mood and each song demands the same flexibility in changing expression as does a group of unrelated songs, one still sings a cycle within a single frame. It is *one* fate, *one* life, *one* single chain of experience, of joys and sorrows, which, when united, seem indivisible.

This is a very great task for a singer.

Before beginning to study a cycle, immerse yourself with your whole being in the figure into which you will transform yourself, to whom you will give life with these songs. You must love this central figure of your cycle, you must be one with it, be happy and sad with it, live and die with it.

When I mention not being interrupted by applause as an advantage, I do not mean to say anything against applause as such. On the contrary, an artist needs the response of his audience, he needs confirmation, he needs the intoxication which comes with the feeling that he is understood. He does not want to experience the exaltation of these hours alone, he wants to sense the deep communion which comes of feeling one with his audience. He would like to take them all to his heart, knowing that they understand and like him, that they enjoy his singing as he enjoys this feeling of participation. It is applause which makes this possible.

But in a cycle, in order to illuminate the figure whom you represent, you must explore it psychologically. Through song sketches you must portray a human being, you must build up and consummate the fate of that human being. It requires enormous concentration to achieve this.

8

Applause between individual songs would destroy the inner absorption. It is for you to make certain that you are not interrupted by applause by holding your listeners bound as if under a spell. Stand motionless between the songs; permit yourself no relaxation. Hold the mood of the song which you have just ended until the beginning of the following one. The intervals between the songs can only be very brief—you will soon develop an instinctive feeling as to when to pause and when to continue. When a cycle is completed, the breaking of the spell under which you have sung it leaves you in a state of exhaustion which seems almost unbearable. But it is the wonderful exhaustion which the creator feels when he has completed a work of art and realizes that it is good, that he has given it life with his own breath, his own heart, his own soul.

There are cycles in which the songs are not interrelated, but are the work of one poet. It is his creative mind which binds together what, as a story, does not belong together, as, for example, Schumann's *Liederkreis*.

Then there are those where there is no single poet to link together unrelated ideas. Yet I have added to my cycles Schubert's *Schwanengesang*, for these Lieder are the last which Schubert wrote. They are his final legacy to the world of music, and to the singers who will bring them to life.

In conclusion, I would like to add a note about accompanists and about 'orchestral' song cycles.

The importance of an accompanist cannot be overemphasized. The singer must be in complete musical harmony with him, while he must be certain of following every shade of the singer's expression. For me, Paul Ulanowsky was the ideal accompanist, and I have dedicated this book to him in memory of those many hours of mutual pleasure and mutual devotion to the work we were performing. One might perhaps suppose that a great concert pianist would be a wonderful accompanist, but that is not the case. An accompanist must be the servant of a singer. He must, so to speak, play second fiddle and leave the singer completely in charge. This attitude to piano-playing is quite foreign to the concert pianist. His very individuality would destroy the essential harmony between the two interpreters. I once sang at a private concert in Vienna to the accompaniment of a great and distinguished

Viennese pianist, and I had absolutely no inner *rapport* with him. He *played* superbly, but he did not *accompany*.

The ideal thing, of course, is to have the same accompanist on every occasion. I was fortunate enough to find others, besides Ulanowsky, who were in complete sympathy with me; but I was always happiest when Paul Ulanowsky played for me. I was always a singer who avoided the strictly conventional approach. I sometimes altered the shade of expression according to my inner feeling or emotion. In some remarkable way, Ulanowsky would sense this even *before* I sang a particular phrase.

Unfortunately, I was never lucky enough to sing with Gerald Moore, and that is something I have greatly regretted. The sensitive Ivor Newton occasionally played for me at private concerts, and I had the pleasure of having him as my accompanist at my master-classes in interpretation at the Wigmore Hall. It was wonderful how he adapted himself to the different personalities of the young singers.

Finally, a word about song cycles with orchestral accompaniment. Of the cycles which I have included in this book, Strauss' *Vier letzte Lieder* were, of course, composed for voice and orchestra; Wagner's *Wesendoncklieder* and Berlioz' *Nuits d'été* exist with both piano and orchestral accompaniment, although the latter were originally written for voice and small orchestra; Brahms' *Vier ernste Gesänge*, written for voice and piano, have been orchestrated by other hands. And so on.

Purely 'orchestral' Lieder should never be sung to a piano accompaniment, though I must confess that I have often been guilty of so doing. The composer knows better; for him, the vision of a unity which must not be destroyed by the singer.

The natural setting for an orchestral Lied is a great concert hall. There, not only do the surging *crescendi* achieve their full effect, but also the softest *pianissimi* which take on a special floating quality on the wings of the orchestra.

I find it quite appalling that before the First World War a German firm issued records in which Lieder, which were written for voice and piano, were given an orchestral 'background'. For example, I had to sing Schumann's *Frauenliebe und -Leben* with orchestra, and the very thought makes me blush today. Such is the power of a great firm over a young beginner!

In this book I have not distinguished between songs written with piano or orchestra and have referred simply to 'accompaniment'. Were I to involve myself in orchestral analysis, I should soon find myself out of my depth. There is a proverb which says that a cobbler should stick to his last. I was first and last a *singer* and it is *singing* I am writing about here.

And here I find myself in some difficulty. For how can I readily explain the difference in voice production when one is singing with an orchestra as opposed to a piano? I cannot recall that I used any different technique or, to put it another way, that I sang any 'differently'. I followed my inner feeling and when the waves of orchestral sound surged about me, I probably sang with greater volume. But always, *always*, I sang from the heart, not from technical considerations.

AN DIE FERNE GELIEBTE

LUDWIG VAN BEETHOVEN

Born in Bonn, 16 December 1770. Died Vienna, 26 March 1827. *An die ferne Geliebte* was composed in April, 1816. At that date, Beethoven had already written the first eight of his nine symphonies and all five of his piano concertos. The cycle therefore stands on the threshold of his last period. It is also, historically, the first song cycle and, as such, was greatly to influence Schubert and—24 years later—Schumann.

ALOIS JEITTELES

Born 1794 in Brünn, and died there in 1858. A Doctor of Medicine and editor of the *Brünner Zeitung*, he wrote many comedies which were widely performed, but is remembered today solely for the poems which Beethoven set in this cycle.

As you begin to study *An die ferne Geliebte* you will see that the songs which the poet sings to his beloved, telling of the beauty of spring and of his love and longing for her, are set within the frame of a beautifully simple melody which in its warm and glowing flow gives them a shimmering loveliness apart from their intrinsic quality. The real inner feeling floats through the *frame* of this melody. Here you, the lover, tell of your yearning love. The songs themselves are like flowers which you send to your beloved who is far away. You have placed them within a lovely wreath and sent them as an expression of your devotion.

Auf dem Hügel sitz' ich, spähend

Begin the prelude with full voice and sing the first three verses in a warm floating line. Begin the fourth verse: 'Will denn nichts mehr zu dir dringen' *piano*, with a wistful restraint. Put your whole heart into the phrase 'Singen will ich, Lieder singen'. Make it very clear that it is *here* that you begin to sing the songs themselves. Until now it has been your *heart* which spoke, now it is your *imagination* which is creating the songs for your beloved, because, as you say in the fifth verse, music dissolves the distance which separates you and makes your spirits one. Feeling how near your beloved seems, as you sing to her, a great joy overwhelms you: at 'und ein liebend Herz erreichet' your tempo quickens. With the beginning of the songs be different: the lover who gazed into the distance with melancholy longing, has now changed into the creative artist. Inspiration is now the source of your singing, it is no longer a matter of morbid and passive longing.

Wo die Berge so blau

Begin the first song, 'Wo die Berge so blau', lightly, *un poco allegretto*; the voice must have the quality of soaring. The distance which at first seemed grey and sombre, because it separated you from your beloved, now becomes bright and filled with radiance. Beyond is sunlight and the fog seems but a veil from out of which rise the blue mountains. After the first 'möchte ich sein' which should be sung quite lightly, you pause for a moment in your thoughts: deep in your heart burns your longing—and those words have again awakened the realization of your loneliness. With great emotion, hesitantly, almost tremblingly you repeat: 'möchte ich sein'. Now it is as if you listen to the lovely melody which is floating through your mind—almost mechanically verses rush through your thoughts —but the musical line is stronger, becoming 'song', and the words are only like a whispering sigh. Sing very *pianissimo* the phrases 'dort im ruhigen Tal' and let 'möchte ich sein' almost fade away in a sigh of longing. But then take hold of yourself. You want to be lost again in melancholy, you want to send the flowers of your thoughts to your beloved. So you continue to compose. Twice—caught by the significance of your words— you pause. First at 'innere Pein'. Notice the *sforzato* before the repetition: it is as if something grips your heart. Sing 'innere Pein' with passionate feeling. The second pause is at 'ewiglich sein'. This should be sung as a climax with breadth and longing.

Leichte Segler in den Höhen

The next song is filled with joy and should have a floating quality. You have made up your mind: these should be lovely and light, unburdened songs. They should make her happy, make her smile. Your impatient, glowing heart must be quieted. So begin with a lightly coloured voice. Notice carefully where you must sing a light, almost *staccato* melody and where the *staccato* changes into a soft *legato*. Remember that you want and intend to be light and unburdened and without any sentimentality, but again and again your imagination is overwhelmed by the words or the music, as they bring the image of your beloved before you so vividly, so that you cannot restrain your feeling. Always colour your voice more darkly in the *legato* phrases. For instance: 'Seht ihr Wolken sie dann gehen sinnend' is *staccato*. But now in your imagination you see her walking there and the next phrase, full of emotion and longing, changes from *staccato* to a warm *legato*: 'in dem stillen Tal, lasst mein Bild vor ihr entstehen'—then again light and *staccato* in 'in dem luft'gen Himmelssaal'. This changing interplay continues through the whole song. The *staccati* should not be exaggerated. Sing them lightly and without any hardness.

At the end of the last verse: 'Meine Tränen ohne Zahl' lift your gaze towards the sky, where in the deep blue of the heavens, the windswept clouds, the flying birds, you find inspiration for your wreath of songs. It is as if the fresh wind has lifted from you clouds of melancholy—you feel refreshed, elated, filled with optimism.

Diese Wolken in den Höhen

Sing 'Diese Wolken in den Höhen' with your head thrown back, vividly and filled with enthusiasm. Your voice must have a quality which conveys courage, adventure, delight. It is as if you stand there at the top of the hill, where in the beginning you had sat, sad and discouraged. Now the wind blows through your hair, your eyes sparkle, your blood pulses through your veins.

Es kehret der Maien, es blühet die Au

Now you are able to sing a lovely harmless little song about nature and the pair of swallows under your roof. Your voice should be light and playful: 'Es kehret der Maien, es blühet die Au'. You tell how everyone who loves will find a companion in May, just as the happy swallows do. The natural climax of the song would be to end it with the blissful thought: 'and so we shall be united'. But you cannot say this. You realize that the song must end with disharmony. Everyone else is united, only I am caught here while my beloved is far away! Darkness falls upon you again. Slowly you sink back and tears run down your cheeks. Sing with a long *ritardando*: 'und Tränen sind all' ihr Gewinnen'.

In creating these songs you have unburdened your heart. You are not happy but you are less miserable than you were.

17

You feel sure that your beloved will be delighted to receive these songs which were inspired by your longing for her and this thought gives you satisfaction.

Nimm sie hin denn, diese Lieder

The frame closes around your songs. Now it is again your heart which speaks; sitting on the hilltop in the glow of evening, a feeling of peace pervades you. Sing with a quiet dignity: 'Nimm sie hin denn, diese Lieder'. Your voice is rich and warm. Give it a quality which may convey the loveliness of this scene: 'Wenn das Dämmerungsrot dann ziehet'. Feel the beauty of these words and the incredible beauty of the musical line. Spin out the *ritardando* in a soft *pianissimo* to 'Bergeshöh'. The words 'und du singst' should be in broad *adagio*, filled with a growing delight. You picture your beloved in all her beauty singing the songs which you have written for her. This is an overwhelming thought. Continue very simply and spin out the *crescendo*: 'nur der Sehnsucht sich bewusst' with *ritenuto* up to a *subito piano* at 'bewusst'.

The melody which follows is, until the end, like a joyful hymn of reunion. You cannot be together in reality, but you are united in soul and in spirit. Sing this whole verse exultantly and feel the victorious delight which the music expresses until the very end. The *diminuendo* in the postlude is like a smiling greeting, like a caressing, happy thought.

DIE SCHÖNE MÜLLERIN

FRANZ SCHUBERT

Born 1797 in the Liechtental suburb of Vienna. Died in Vienna, 1828. *Die schöne Müllerin* was composed during 1823, when Schubert was simultaneously working on his opera *Fierrabras*, and was published in five instalments during 1824.

WILHELM MÜLLER

Born in Dessau, 1794, and died there in 1827. He was therefore an almost exact contemporary of Schubert. His poetry was greatly influenced by the Romantic spirit of such works as *Des Knaben Wunderhorn*, but he is remembered today only for *Die schöne Müllerin* and for *Die Winterreise*, the cycle of poems which Schubert set in 1827.

The young miller has said farewell to the master in whose mill he has been working and has once again set forth upon his way as a wandering apprentice.

I remember from my childhood these lads, who, covered with dust and often hungry and exhausted, used to pass our home which lay on the road between Hamburg and Berlin. I can still see these young figures vividly before me, when I picture the miller boy of this cycle, but he must have been a very unusual one. For he is shy and sensitive and there is the soul of a poet in the dreamer who loves to wander through the world, enjoying its beauties with open eyes. There is the soul of the dreamer who is destined to be wounded, for it is too sensitive, too vulnerable, too unprepared for the bitter disillusionments of life.

But at the beginning of the cycle, a radiant sky still shines upon his road. He strides along his way, free from care, with a gay song upon his lips.

DAS WANDERN

Begin with a buoyant tempo as if you were wandering along briskly and were enjoying looking around you. You sing of the things which most concern you: of your world, which is the long country road stretching out before you, white and shimmering: the gaily chattering brook, whirring windmills, grinding millstones. In each verse you should picture differently the things which you describe as you wander along, singing happily. Give your voice a light, mysterious quality as you speak of water, for the murmuring brook has always had a rather strange attraction for you, sing gaily and with a quickened tempo of the tirelessly turning wheels and with a whimsical clumsiness of the dancing, ponderous stones. In the last verse your recurrent farewell to the master and the mistress is without any sadness, even free of any regret. You are just a young apprentice, you work where you find a mill and go upon your way singing happily.

WOHIN?

You wander through forests and meadows and over wooded hills, wherever your path may lead you. Somewhere, sometime, you know you will come upon a mill and find work and good friends. So you wander on confidently, filled with the joy of living. But suddenly your footsteps halt: you hear the murmur of a brook—and there, before you, you see a fresh mountain spring gushing out between the stones. Splashing gaily, it dashes down the hillside towards the valley. With your eyes you follow the silver shimmer of its falling waters. It is so lovely here among the mountains and you feel so fresh and free. The wind plays through your blond hair and cools your moist brow. But the brook seems to lure you, strangely. Its rippling murmur seems to say: 'Follow me!'

Begin this song as if you were listening to something which is far away. You should have an expression of excited concentration as if it is something strange which you hear. Sing 'ich weiss nicht, wie mir wurde' in a restrained *piano*, as if with amazement. 'Hinunter und immer weiter' should be slightly *accelerando* as if driven by a power which you must obey. (One must immediately sense in this song the peculiar connection between you and the brook which becomes your friend and companion, your counsellor—and finally your grave.)

The brook becomes wider, its rippling more distinct—and you follow its course, led on as if under its spell. Sing 'ist das denn meine Strasse?' as if you are confused. Ask this as a confused child would, with uncertainty and amazement. But sing 'du hast mit deinem Rauschen mir ganz berauscht den Sinn' joyfully and without concern. Your romantic imagination enjoys this strange feeling of being led away from your path. The flow of your romantic imagination sweeps on: it must be water sprites, lovely alluring water sprites who sing their seductive songs to you. Sing this lightly, with a feeling of mystery; but smiling as if in play, your thoughts take the form of verses. You wander happily along the brook, knowing that sometime, somewhere, it will lead you to a mill. Let the end of the song fade away, as if the wandering figure of the young miller is merging into the blue distance.

HALT

Take up immediately, in a happy mood, the lively tempo of the prelude: you see before you a wonderful mill, and after the freedom of your wandering the thought of working appeals to you again. Begin with joyful excitement: 'Eine Mühle seh' ich blinken' and sing 'bricht Rädergebraus' with a surging *crescendo* like a billowing wave. 'Ei willkommen, süsser Mühlengesang!' is a warm greeting—sing it vivaciously, with radiant happiness. Seeing the freshly painted house, with its windows flashing in the sunlight, you take it to your heart. Sing with overflowing joy. And gratefully you think of the stream, whose seductive murmur has led you here. Sing with delicacy and with a smile 'Ei Bächlein, liebes Bächlein, war es also gemeint?'

DANKSAGUNG AN DEN BACH

Now you have found your mill, you have work which you enjoy, and a place in this lovely house in which you feel at home. For all this you have your brook to thank, which led you away from your intended path. But it seems, you have still more to be grateful for: the miller has a lovely daughter. . . . And you have fallen very much in love with her.

Begin with great warmth but nevertheless with an expression of delighted roguishness: 'War es also gemeint, mein rauschender Freund?' 'Gelt, hab' ich's verstanden' should be sung as if you share a secret with the brook. Let the word 'gelt' stand alone, making a short pause after this word so that it stands as if separated from the question. 'Hat sie dich geschickt oder hast mich berückt?' should be sung very softly and shyly. Your poetic imagination would so gladly let you believe that it was the wish of the lovely miller's maid which sang to you from out of the rippling of the brook. But you know that it cannot be so. And your acceptance of reality is smiling and filled with expectancy. Sing 'Nach Arbeit ich frug, nun hab' ich genug für die Hände, für's Herze' happily and with the confidence of youth which is able to see everything around it in a rosy light. Make a slight pause before 'Für's Herze', sing this rather whimsically and with a tender boldness and close with 'Vollauf genug' as if you wanted to say: 'Yes, it is enough, but I know that something far lovelier awaits me. . . .'

FEIERABEND

But your impetuous heart puts an end to your happy contentment. You are young, you are healthy, you seek love and close companionship. With great zest you throw yourself into your daily work—you want to show her how you woo her with your whole soul, how you want to belong to her, to work for her, to spoil her and to love her.

Take up the *molto allegro* of the prelude, stand very erect, with flashing eyes, as if ready to struggle and determined to win. Begin with glowing impatience, impetuously and forcefully: 'Hätt' ich tausend Arme zu rühren'. Sing 'was ich hebe, was ich trage' almost with despair, but there should be no tragedy in this. It is the despairing impatience of one in love, which causes the bystander some quiet amusement. Be a little quieter in tempo at 'und da sitz' ich in der grossen Runde', but do not drag the tempo. Colour your voice more darkly when the master says 'euer Werk hat mir gefallen', sing this with a broad ponderousness as if you want to imitate the words of the master. Then immediately colour your voice more brightly at 'und das liebe Mädchen sagt'. Sing the first 'allen eine gute Nacht' *pianissimo*, see before you the lovely girl, how she stands at the door, smiling, delighting everyone with her friendly greeting. But the *sforzato* in the accompaniment is the piercing thought: she says it to everyone, she is indifferent to me, for her I am only one of them—she sends me no special greeting. Sing the second 'allen' with a pained expression. The accompaniment breaks in dramatically upon your words and you again sing with the same passionate impatience as at the beginning of this song. Sing the last 'dass die schöne Müllerin' slightly *ritardando* and *piano*, delicately and very longingly. End with great feeling and a dreamy yearning: 'merkte meinen treuen Sinn'. With the two final chords of the postlude, you awaken again to the uncertainty of reality.

DER NEUGIERIGE

You are a shy boy and the love for the miller's daughter which has filled your heart so suddenly and so overwhelmingly has made you still more shy. You have found no friend among the other miller boys, your heart is too heavy with your love, you cannot be carefree and gay as they are. So you become lonely and strange. You have never played or danced or drunk with the others in your free time, no, you have gone your lonely way, always near the brook. Today you are again beside it. Your heart is filled with love, with hope and shy expectation. If only you could be sure that your love has its echo in the heart of the maiden! You thought you saw a happy answer in her eyes, but perhaps you only imagined that she looked at you lovingly. If only you knew whom you could ask! Being too shy to ask her yourself, you long for some confirmation. But to whom could you go? Certainly not to her father or to the other boys. So you sit there alone—and lonely.

In the prelude is your question: whom could I ask? You look hesitantly about you. Your face has a dreaming expression. Sing with a tender softness until 'ich erführ' so gern'. Then there comes a subtle change: you explain to yourself why neither the flowers nor the stars will give you an answer. You are not a gardener and so you cannot understand the voice of the flowers. The stars are too high above you, how could you hear their melodies? But there is always your friend, the brook. He will answer you. He spoke to you as you were wandering along your way. He brought you here, he will know. He will tell you if your heart is right—your heart which tells you that she loves you. You listen to the short prelude—and to the silence of the silent bar. But the brook gives no answer. Begin now with a soft reproach—*molto lento* and *piano*. Sing with a beautiful floating *legato*. The dreaming smile should never leave your face. You are so hopeful, you are almost certain that your heart does not betray you. If you were really afraid of the answer you would not ask your question in such a dreamlike way. You would be more urgent and passionate.

'Ja, heisst das eine Wörtchen' is filled with happiness, but do not sing it too loudly. It should be like a soft, happy sigh.

25

Make a slight pause before 'nein' in the next phrase, as if you hesitate even to *think* that there might be a possibility of a 'no'. The crescendo in 'die beiden Wörtchen schliessen' is like a soft surging wave and subsides into a breathy *pianissimo* in 'die ganze Welt mir ein' and in the repetition of it.

In the interlude you are again listening to the brook. But the waters only sing their own melody—there is no answer to your question. Imagine that you are bending down nearer to the brook as if you want to tell it a secret or are urging it to share a secret with you. ('Will's ja nicht weiter sagen . . .') Hiding your face from the outer world as you bend down over the softly murmuring brook, you dare, for the first time, to voice your inner hope, to ask the question which is burning within your heart: 'sag' Bächlein, liebt sie mich?' Make a lovely climax at 'liebt', but do not sing it too loudly. Intensity of expression is here much more effective than a booming *forte*. The repetition of the last phrase should be sung as if you are overwhelmed by happiness. Even saying aloud that she may love you, even just saying it, makes you tremble with joy. Your expression should remain unchanged until the end of the postlude.

UNGEDULD

Your trembling, throbbing heart beats in a stormy tempo through this song. Sing with a fiery impetuosity, and very distinctly. The lively animated tempo and the exact rhythm of the dotted notes continue without cessation from the beginning until the end of the song. The more rhythmically you sing, the more you will succeed in bringing out the feverish impatience of the throbbing heartbeats. In each verse from out of the surging restlessness there blooms, in a broad line and with great feeling, the confession of your devotion: 'Dein ist mein Herz und soll es ewig bleiben'.

(Incidentally, I always sang only three verses, the first, second and fourth.)

MORGENGRUSS

Shyly and humbly you approach the window of your beloved. It is a lovely warm summer morning and you long to greet her and look up towards her window. But she vanishes behind the curtains, after convincing herself with a hasty look that it is you who stands expectantly upon her threshold.

But the look which she threw you could not have been unfriendly, for you begin the song in a mood of happy animation. Sing whimsically and gaily: 'Guten Morgen, schöne Müllerin'. You do not really mean seriously the question 'Verdriesst dich denn mein Gruss so schwer? Verstört dich denn mein Blick so sehr?' You sing this more in a teasing way and add roguishly 'so muss ich wieder gehen'.

The second verse should be sung with a tender intimacy. In the shyness of your heart you look without any desire to your beloved: 'O lass' mich nur von ferne steh'n'. Sing pleadingly 'du blondes Köpfchen, komm hervor'; and then very rapturously 'ihr blauen Morgensterne'. I have always omitted the third verse, but if you sing it, sing it softly and dreamily.

The last verse is somewhat more lively in tempo, very fresh and soaring. End the song *piano*, softly, with a slight *ritardando*.

DES MÜLLERS BLUMEN

You bring flowers to her bedroom window and plant them where they may bloom in the light of her eyes. This song flows along in a lovely *moderato*. Avoid throughout giving too equal emphasis to every syllable and in this way making this beautiful song monotonous. It is important that you recite the poem, so that you get the feeling of these floating phrases in speaking and so make it easier to achieve the same effect in singing them. Lift out the important word in each phrase with a discreet emphasis and sing towards it and away from it with a softly floating swing. 'Ihr wisst ja was ich meine' should be very *pianissimo* and should be sung with a subtle delicacy.

In the third verse the musical phrase continues while the verbal phrase must make a slight pause. Make this necessary pause very discreetly without disturbing the musical line.

Sing the last verse with deep feeling. With the flowers, you give her the tears which you weep because of her, of her who seems so far beyond your reach. Sing very softly and with inner trembling: 'der Tau in euren Äugelein, das sollen meine Tränen sein, die will ich auf euch weinen'.

TRÄNENREGEN

This song must be sung with deep emotion. Feel the subtle poetry in both the words and the music. With the beginning of the prelude feel the dreaming enchantment of the moonlit night. Sing very tenderly, in a swinging *legato* and very distinctly. 'Wir schauten so traulich zusammen hinab in den rieselnden Bach' should be sung as if in your thoughts you are bending down over the brook. Give an especial significance to 'rieselnden Bach'. It is the brook which has lured you to this mill—the brook to whom you now feel close in an hour which may perhaps be decisive for your whole life. You are alone with your adored one, the magic of the quiet moonlit night envelops you, perhaps you will find the courage to ask the question which will decide whether your life is to be one of joy or sorrow. Sing with a dreamy delight: 'Der Mond war auch gekommen, die Sternlein hinterdrein.'

Sing the second verse with a somewhat more animated tempo, with restraint but with glowing feeling. There is a surging warmth and a tender restraint in 'Ich schaute nach ihrem Bilde, nach ihren Augen allein'. You are so young and shy. You do not dare to look into the face of your beloved as she sits beside you, no, you look down into the brook in which her beauty is mirrored. Sing with a rapturous, dreamlike quality: 'und sahe sie nicken und blicken herauf aus dem seligen Bach'. You believe the brook is blissfully happy because it holds the image of your beloved within its water.

Begin the third verse as if in mystified astonishment: 'Und in den Bach versunken der ganze Himmel schien . . .' You see the deep blue heaven with its brilliant stars reflected in the brook. Heaven and water seem mysteriously interwoven, the earth seems extinguished, you yourself seem to soar over the strange picture of the heavens, over the brook and the image of your beloved, between stars and clouds. This vision grips your thirsty, impressionable, vulnerable, poet's soul. Confusion sweeps over you—the beauty of this moment is too great, too much for you. You lean down towards the brook and see its waters, like a luminous veil, rippling on over the image of your beloved, over heaven and its stars. 'Und über den Wolken und

Sternen da rieselte munter der Bach'. Sing this with delighted amazement but at the same time with restraint. And sing mysteriously, calling and yet listening: 'und rief mit Singen und Klingen: Geselle, Geselle! mir nach'. Lift out the two words 'Geselle, Geselle' like a call, sing them separated from the continuing musical phrase and give them a quality of uncanniness. The brook is calling you. Does it call you away from here? Does it want you to follow it and wander on along a carefree road, away from the girl whom you love and in whose hands rests your fate? Or does it call you down? Does it want you to be lost in the reflected image as it closes over you?

This moment decides your fate . . .

In your confusion you do not understand the warning of the brook. You do not obey its admonition—you stay. But instead of taking the girl into your arms, as she perhaps expected and hoped you would, you bow your head, and tears of confusion start to fall.

The girl's nature is a completely prosaic one, the overpowering emotion of the youth at her side is to her something foreign and beyond her understanding. She looks at him with a mixture of scorn, compassion and fear. He seems strange to her. Suddenly she gets up and the only thing which she can think of saying in this hour of enchantment is the very prosaic remark: 'Es kommt ein Regen, ade, ich geh' nach Haus . . .' ('It's going to rain, good-bye, I'm going home') Sing this *piano*, rather impatiently, but with a suggestion of fear and a little scorn. In this one sentence you must convey the picture of the girl: an unromantic, commonplace nature, coquettish, a little superior, scornful but at the same time almost superstitiously fearful of anything which is at all foreign to her. And that the miller lad, this dreaming, unworldly poet, certainly is.

In the postlude slowly bow your head as if you, the miller boy, are withdrawing into yourself.

MEIN!

But one day you found the courage to ask the question which has obsessed you for so long a time. The answer made you unspeakably happy—the answer was the longed for 'yes'.

Perhaps no one had ever before spoken to the girl in the way you did. Perhaps your poetic spirit found the right words with which to touch her heart, the small and commonplace heart of one who can only feel superficially, but which you in your flowering imagination have clothed with beauty. Perhaps in this moment she had loved you as much as it was possible for her to love. Happiness flooded through you like a stream of gold. In the surge of your emotion, you are confused and helpless as never before in your life. You would like to hold fast the current of time, to change the whole everyday world into one resounding, soaring symphony which would sing only of your joy and on the wings of its song would carry your ecstasy to the sun itself.

This song should be given a very quick tempo. It is like one breathless avalanche of word and sound. Immediately take up the storm of the prelude, plunge with your whole being into the turbulent music. But do not sing loudly. Begin with exalted excitement. Build up! The first *forte* is at 'mein' and sing the following 'mein', which is broadly spun out, with full and exultant power.

The whole middle part of the song should be sung with great restraint, but quickly, as if in a rapturous whisper.

Without slowing the tempo, end with an exultant *fortissimo*. Hold the tension until the end of the postlude.

This song is a very difficult one. It will take a long time before you can give it quite the right form. To convey vehemence of expression and yet be at the same time restrained is especially difficult. But you *must* accomplish this, for otherwise this whole song will become an undifferentiated *forte* and will lose its essential character, which must be one of blissful confusion. It would become commonplace and that is something which should be very far from the miller boy. Try to imagine singing as if you are intoxicated—imagine that your whole body sways, as it would for example if sitting in a soaring swing. You become one with its motion. So let yourself be carried by the swing of these phrases. The whole world is your swing.

PAUSE

It is as if weariness overcomes you after the tumult of the first overpowering storm of happiness. You seem to be in a dream. Now that your beloved has said 'yes', there should be nothing which could depress you. You should now be deeply contented and completely happy. But the burden of joy is almost more than you can bear and in the depths of your soul is the fear, which you will not admit even to yourself, that such happiness cannot really be lasting. Why should you think this? Why can you not enjoy your happiness completely? You feel the true nature of your beloved, you see her superficially, and even if you do close your eyes and try with your whole heart to believe in her, there is still in the depths of your soul a kernel of unrest.

Begin the prelude quietly, looking up. Your facial expression should convey a deep awareness of your happiness, your smile is full of contentment and devotion. (Do not drag this song; the tempo is *moderato* and it should not be made sentimental.)

Sing quietly: 'Meine Laute hab' ich gehängt an die Wand' and sing: 'ich kann nicht mehr singen' with suppressed passion. An inner amazement sounds through the words—'Ei, wie gross ist wohl meines Glückes Last.' Always in your life you have found words and when alone have been able to express in poetry whatever moved you. All the suffering of your young life became poetry, but now happiness makes you mute. This seems very strange to you and fills you with astonishment.

Sing the beginning of the second verse with great tenderness. You speak to the lute as if it were your friend. It has always been with you. It has accompanied you in all your wanderings, it has carried your complaints and all your yearning songs. Now it seems as if you are separated from a beloved being, who is silent at the moment when you long to hear its voice. As if with a delicate touch, your words stroke the lute—'nun, liebe Laute, ruh' an dem Nagel hier'. Sing very delicately 'und streift eine Biene mit ihren Flügeln dich'. Here again you must understand how to paint with word and tone: sing this line with a gentle swing, making the bees which buzz around the strings of the lute seem alive. 'Da wird mir so bange und es durchschauert mich' should be sung *ritenuto* with a strange and restrained anxiety. Your glance is clouded during the short interlude. Look as if you were searching in the distance, anxiously questioning. The question 'Warum liess ich das Band auch hängen so lang?' must have an uncanny quality.

You fear something, but you bury your head so that you cannot see it, you refuse to recognize that there is something which you should fear. You are not a fighter. For you there can be no challenge, you will never look into the face of fate with flashing eager eyes as so many young people of your age would enjoy doing. No, you want to hide in order to protect your sensitive spirit.

Listen again to the distance from which seem to come disquieting voices. Strangely you sometimes seem to hear a sigh trembling through the strings of the beloved lute. It makes you shudder. Sing with restraint and heavily the pressing question: 'Ist es der Nachklang meiner Liebespein?' How you wish it might be—but you are not sure. Very softly, trembling and with great restraint you ask the fatal question: 'Soll es das Vorspiel neuer Lieder sein?' (Remember that in the past it has only been pain, loneliness, longing which has brought you songs. In happiness they have never come to you. What you want to say is: 'or will I again be abandoned and lonely and filled with longing and so again be able to sing my songs?') The new songs bode no good. It is a premonition of sorrow and pain which trembles through you. And yet you love your songs. Even though they may be born from pain you love them and in your happiness have missed them. So in the last repetition of the question—'Soll es das Vorspiel neuer Lieder sein?'—let there be a subtle expression of pained happiness. Even though grief should overwhelm you, you will still have your songs.

MIT DEM GRÜNEN LAUTENBAND

This is one of the few songs in this cycle (and in any case, the last one) which has a carefree quality. You have thrust aside the lurking premonition; you are living completely in the happy present. Your loved one has been with you and has seen the pretty green ribbon which was tied upon your lute. She was eager to have this ribbon to decorate her dress and her hair. Everything about your beloved gives you delight. That she will rob your lute of its adornment in order to place the ribbon upon her hair is like a command for you. You take the ribbon from the lute and send it to her. Green is her favourite colour. Green is becoming to her. This green which later becomes the hated colour (the coat of the hunter, with whom the unfaithful one betrays you, is green) now seems the most beautiful colour in the world to you, because she loves it. (Perhaps she has said that she loves green because she has already flirted with the handsome hunter. Perhaps it is a tragic farce that you, the poor miller boy, share her preference for green. Perhaps she is already laughing secretly. Who knows? ...) Sing this song with freshness and as if you are free of every care. You are filled with optimism, you sing playfully and whimsically. Avoid any suggestion of heaviness here, sing with warmth of feeling and with inner delight. End the song with a happy air of confidence.

DER JÄGER

The realization that your beloved is not averse to the attentions of the hunter has come as a shock to you, for you could not burst out in the violent passion which speaks from this song if you were entirely sure of your beloved. This is no jealousy born of anger at the daring of one who pursues the girl whom you consider yours. No, it is the jealousy of the man who fears that he might lose his beloved to the other one.

The whole song should be sung with a wildness which is entirely foreign to the nature of the gentle miller boy. But the shock has been too great. You have been torn too suddenly from your dreams, which were almost unbearably beautiful. You have been wounded to the quick. Sing the whole song from beginning to end in a violent tempo. It is especially important to enunciate distinctly in this song. In singing you must *recite* this song. End with great bitterness, with trembling contempt: 'und treten und wühlen herum in dem Feld, die Eber, die schiesse, du Jägerheld'. This should be sung between the teeth with a distorted expression, almost through tears of rage.

EIFERSUCHT UND STOLZ

But from the hunter who seems scarcely worth your contempt you turn back to your beloved: you can no longer deny to yourself that she is the guilty one, that it is she who has betrayed you and has turned her fickle heart to the hunter. It is a sign of your inner loneliness that you now take refuge again with the brook, the one friend to whom you may confess your feelings. You see in its vigorous flow the wish to revenge you. You believe that the brook, your friend, wants to pursue the hunter who has robbed you of your happiness. The splashing waves which at the beginning of the cycle, when you were still carefree and happy, sang a gay wanderer's song to you, now sing the words of your heart, that heart which was once so good and kind but has now learned to hate and longs for revenge.

Begin the song with deep excitement. Sing with marked accentuation, noting the dotted notes exactly. They again give the impression of the throbbing of your heart. Sing 'kehr' um, kehr' um,' with violent passion. 'Ihren leichten, losen, kleinen Flattersinn' should be sung as if with suppressed pain. It is touching that you still try to think of the failings of your beloved as if they were simply a whim, which springs not from ill will but from the fact that she is really nothing more than a child and so to be excused. You want to deceive yourself, to excuse what cannot be excused. But you love her so much—you still cannot believe that she is really lost to you—not yet. . . . Sing as if you were telling the brook a secret: 'Sahst du sie gestern Abend nicht am Tore steh'n' and sing 'Wenn von dem Fang der Jäger lustig zieht nach Haus, da steckt kein sittsam Kind den Kopf zum Fenster 'naus,' with the somewhat reproachful tone of an older person who is annoyed by the follies of youth. Sing in the same way 'Geh' Bächlein hin und sag' ihr das.' You must talk in a very intimate way with the brook as if it were really an understanding friend. Sing 'Doch sag' ihr nicht, hörst du, kein Wort' in a whisper almost *parlando*, cut the 'nicht' very short and lift out 'hörst du'. Sing softly and very *legato* 'von meinem traurigen Gesicht'—pour your whole grief into these words, all your despair, your bitter disillusionment must echo through them. Sing 'sag' ihr' as if you were considering what message you would give the brook for your beloved—and sing 'Er schnitzt bei mir sich eine Pfeif' aus Rohr' as if it were a sudden decision. Sing this with a bitter smile of superiority, as if you wanted to give the impression that you *are* quite superior and have not the slightest intention of taking the unfaithfulness of your beloved as though it were a personal tragedy. Give the impression of still greater indifference in 'und bläst den Kindern schöne Tänz' und Lieder vor', sing this with a swing as if you wanted to make her think that you too have an urge to dance. End with an expression of wildness, singing as if through tears: 'sag' ihr's, sag' ihr's. . . .'

DIE LIEBE FARBE

A sombre longing for death sounds from out of this sorrowful song. The colour green (the colour which in Germany is used for hunters' coats) becomes for you an *idée fixe*: you have realized what a tragi-comic role you must have played in the eyes of your beloved, when you admired this colour with her and agreed that green was your favourite colour too. Perhaps, you think, with the burning distrust of one who has been deceived, it has given her a malicious pleasure to hear you in all your innocence rave about this colour, which she loves because of her dashing hunter. The insignificant episode of the hour in which she asked you for this ribbon attains a torturing significance for you, it pursues you, it scoffs at you, it makes you restless and embittered, you who were such a short time ago the gay and charming, innocently happy young miller lad.

In the prelude emerge as if from sombre thoughts, slowly lift your bowed head and look into the distance with a pained and melancholy expression. Begin to sing in a soft voice as if in a dream, beneath a veil. In this verse sing 'mein Schatz hat's Grün so gern' each time with a mixture of pain and scorn. Colour your voice darkly, sing exceptionally *legato* and very quietly. At 'eine Haide voll grünen Rosmarein' sing a *subito pianissimo* and end the first verse with bitterness: 'mein Schatz hat's Grün so gern'.

The second verse is somewhat more animated. Sing with deep scorn: 'mein Schatz hat's Jagen so gern'. Sing *crescendo* until the end of the repetition of this phrase, then sing *subito piano*—'Das Wild, das ich jage, das ist der Tod'. Close very softly, with tragic bitterness: 'mein Schatz hat's Jagen so gern'.

Begin the third verse in a whispered *piano*, trembling, through tears. This whole verse has no *crescendo*, no *decrescendo*, it flows in a sad monotony as if through tears which smother your voice. Try here to unite the realism of the expression with the melodic line of the song. End with a breathy sigh, through tears. Remain standing quiet and rigid until the postlude dies away.

DIE BÖSE FARBE

You cannot escape from the obsession: the colour green pursues you, mocks at you, will kill you. Your mind begins to be confused. Your delicate and sensitive soul cannot withstand the bitter disillusionment that has come through the realization that this love, this torturing love could be destroyed. Wherever you might flee, the colour green is there—the forest, the fields, the banks of the brook—everything glows at you with this malicious green, driving you mad.

Take up the wild storming of the prelude with your whole being: stand a little bent as if on the point of running away, your facial expression is confused, you give the impression that you are being hunted. Sing with great violence, like a cry of fear: 'Ich möchte flieh'n in die Welt hinaus, hinaus in die weite Welt' and whisper with an expression of insanity— 'wenn's nur so grün nicht wär da draussen in Wald und Feld . . .' The next phrase, 'Ich möchte die grünen Blätter all' pflücken von jedem Zweig' is again like a cry of fear—and 'ich möchte die grünen Gräser all' weinen ganz totenbleich' is again whispered with a hint of madness, mounting to a *fortissimo* outburst at 'bleich'. The short repetition 'weinen ganz totenbleich' should be sung with strong accentuation. Again begin *piano*: 'Ach Grün, du böse Farbe du, was siehst mich immer an so stolz, so keck, so schadenfroh, mich armen, armen weissen Mann?' Sing this with suppressed trembling, with the fear of a madman who believes that he is being pursued. Looking around with an expression of shyness, sing: 'armen, armen weissen Mann' as if through tears. You feel so small, so worthless, beside the pompous, self-confident hunter, who looks still more handsome in his green coat.

The next verse should be sung with an entirely different

expression: with great warmth and emotion, with the whole wonderful humility of a pure heart. Only at the end make a slight *crescendo* at 'das eine Wörtchen Ade'. The next phrases should be sung in very strict rhythm (you should of course always sing rhythmically. If I mention it especially here, it is because the rhythm should be emphasized). It is as if with quick, stealthy steps you hasten to her bedroom window only to see *her*, who has made you so unspeakably unhappy. But what you see fills you with pain. About her brow is tied the green ribbon, the ribbon from your lute which you have given her and which she now uses to adorn herself for another. Sing with vehemence, with an expression of madness: 'O binde von der Stirn dir ab das grüne Band'.

End the song with the same violence, singing 'Ade, ade, und reiche mir zum Abschied deine Hand, zum Abschied deine Hand' as if running away, as if running straight to your death.

TROCKNE BLUMEN

Your longing for death has now changed into a determination to die. Imagine that you are sitting alone, as always, in your little room. In your hands you hold the dried flowers which she had once given you and which you have cherished, perhaps laying them between the pages of your old Bible. Now you take them in your hands as if they were a precious legacy, as if in this hour of leavetaking from all earthly possessions you must decide what is to become of your belongings, as you would about a great and important estate. But there is no one worthy of receiving these flowers which have been your most cherished possession, a token of the short period of happiness that now lies in ruins behind you. You cannot part from them, even in death, so you must take them with you to your grave.

Begin already in the two bars of the prelude to feel the tired, resigned, powerless movement with which you would take the flowers in your hands. Raise your head slowly as if emerging from a deep dream. Your glance is veiled, withdrawn from reality—you are only alive now in the consideration of the withered flowers in your hand. Sing with deep melancholy, very softly and in a veiled *piano*: 'Ihr Blümlein alle, die sie mir gab, euch soll man legen mit mir in's Grab'. Sing a delicate *ritardando* at 'ihr Blümlein alle, wovon so nass?' Hold the word 'nass' and break it off as if your heart has stopped beating. Tears run down your cheeks (in your imagination). Tears moisten the dried flowers in your hand. But the green will never again return to their withered leaves, just as love will never again smile upon you. Sing with deep feeling: 'Ach, Tränen, machen nicht maiengrün, machen tote Liebe nicht wieder blüh'n . . .' Close this verse with a soft *ritardando*: 'die Blümlein alle, die sie mir gab'. Emphasize 'sie' as if with an aching sigh. Your facial expression becomes somewhat more animated, a humble and touching joy pervades you as you sing: 'Und wenn sie wandelt am Hügel vorbei und denkt im Herzen: der meint' es treu . . .' It makes you happy to think that when you are dead, she will realize how much you have loved her. Your dried flowers will bloom again in this happiness, they will grow again as in the sunlight of spring and blossom from out of the grave, under whose green mound the truest and purest heart rests from its suffering. Sing with jubilation but at the same time with tenderness and warmth: 'Dann Blümlein alle, heraus, heraus! Der Mai is kommen, der Winter ist aus . . .' Sing the repetitions of these phrases in exactly the same way—only end the song a little more broadly and emphasize 'kommen' and 'Winter' in the broad swing of the phrase.

In the postlude turn your thoughts again to the faded flowers, those pitiful symbols of your brief and deceptive happiness.

DER MÜLLER UND DER BACH

But how can the miller lad fulfill his determination to die without conferring with the brook, his only friend? So he stands upon its bank where his weary steps have carried him and looks down into the depths of the brook as he communes with it. Sing almost without expression in a sombre monotone. Your soul is no longer really on earth. You have finished with life, the world seems dark around you and seems to have dissolved into a mystical distance. The moon, weeping, covers its face; in its shadow the lilies die, and the white angels, who in the evening float through the blue sky on golden clouds, do not want to see your pain and sing to you comforting songs through their tears of compassion, beckoning you to them. You tell all this in one tone as if passing away, you have already escaped from the earth. But the brook, the kind friend, is wise. For a long, long time it has been flowing through the world. It has seen much and learned much and it knows how transitory are the desires and sorrows of this earth, if one can only understand how to raise oneself above them. While the accompaniment breaks away from the dragging monotony of the first part of the song and begins to flow gaily, the brook speaks to the miller lad. It is as if it wanted to say: be still, my boy. Your suffering will pass. Your loving heart will rise above this grief just as a swan soars out of the water into which it had plunged, as if it would never again return. So will your young heart arise again. And a new star will shine upon you and roses will bloom again from the withered and thorny branches and the angels, who today are weeping above you, will come down to earth and you will greet them and will again be happy. Sing these phrases almost playfully, with a light quality of voice. The brook is wise, the brook is cool and clear, the brook cannot realize the fatal wound within your heart. It only knows that it is the way of the world to be happy and to be sad, and knows that everything, everything is transitory—pain as well as joy. Just as the brook chatters, charmingly, gaily, free from care, so you should sing this song of the brook—coolly, clearly, playfully. But the words of nature which knows eternal resurrection can find no way to this heart which is wounded to death. Sing the last verse of this song with deep emotion. Put all the glow, all the warmth of your heart into the phrase: 'Ach Bächlein, liebes Bächlein, du meinst es so gut, ach, Bächlein, aber weisst du, wie Liebe tut?' Sing with infinite longing, with mystical desire, with great restraint, darkly, and as if you are bending nearer and nearer to the brook, drawn with tenderness and kindness into its cool depths. Sing with half closed lips, the words almost fading away: 'Ach, Bächlein, liebes Bächlein, so singe nur zu . . .' In your imagination you sink slowly, very slowly into the brook. Slowly, very slowly the clear blue waters close over you and you lie cradled in its depths, freed of all earthly pain.

DES BACHES WIEGENLIED

Dying, you lie at the bottom of the brook. You feel the waves, which at the edges of the brook splash and ripple their merry song, singing for you an eternal cradle song. Sing swaying gently, give the impression of being released, as with closed eyes you let your body sway almost imperceptibly with the rhythm of the music. Be one, in your thoughts, with the water, feel the blue infinity above you, feel this wonderful, gentle passing away. It is asking much of the singer, you will say, to make all this your own. On the contrary: *Feeling is everything*. You have lived and suffered with the miller boy through an experience which for him—the world-estranged, tender-hearted dreamer—must have led to an end which was *final*. You have learned to love this figure, which you have awakened to life through your singing, your interpretation. You have suffered with him, you have lived through all his bitter tragedy and now you die with him. You feel now how death is taking you into its arms, the cool kind arms with which the brook, your friend, embraces you. Feel here the sweet painlessness of death—and you will find the right expression for this last song which is a comforting and wonderful requiem. Sing with a darkly coloured voice, but softly as if in a dream. There should be a great surge at 'bis das Meer will trinken die Bächlein aus'. There is a deep joy in this surge of feeling: the ocean, the endless ocean which you have never seen, will drink the brook and with it will take you into itself, will roll you in its great waves from continent to continent, will make you one with the endless infinity of distance.

I always sang only three verses, the first, third and fifth. If you want to sing them all, each one should be painted differently. But never, as you sing, forget that it is a dreamer who is passing away. Never be rigid in your expression. Everything must be subdued, restrained, dreamlike. When in the third verse you sing of the hunting horn, it must be something very distant and unreal. Only the waves which enfold you are reality, they are the *only* reality. Sing the last verse more slowly, and let it be still slower towards the end but never drag in this song. Sing 'Der Vollmond steigt, der Nebel weicht' with a withdrawn expression, very veiled, very mysterious, very unworldly. The ending—'Und der Himmel da oben, wie ist er so weit'—should be trembling, silvery, absolutely ethereal. Soar away with this ending—dissolving, dying this sweet death which makes you one with beauty and with the blue of eternal distance until far, far away you merge with light itself.

DIE WINTERREISE

FRANZ SCHUBERT

WILHELM MÜLLER

Die Winterreise was composed in two parts, the first in February and the second in October, 1827. The first part was published in January, 1828 and the second in December of that year, one month after the composer's death on 19 November.

This cycle is certainly one of the most beautiful which has ever been written. Its origin has been so well described by Newman Flower, that I quote him directly: 'Müller was brilliant in the tone painting of his words. He had a rare sense of humanity. He set down with the most natural ease the atmosphere of a life. "I can neither play nor sing," he wrote. "But when I compose my poem I sing all the same and play as well. If I could express the tunes that come to me, my songs would please better than they do now. But, patience. There may be found a sympathetically tuned soul, which will discover the tunes in the words, and give them back to me."

'Unknowingly he found that soul in Schubert. The last twelve songs in the *Winterreise* cycle show the gloom gathering about him, the infinite sadness which, with the end of all endeavour approaching, had taken its hold on Schubert at the time he composed them. Müller died in September, 1827; Schubert was to set his last songs and pass on little more than a year later. The last *Winterreise* songs are an epic in sadness, the blending of two moods of beauty—both in verse and in music— overshadowed by death.'

This cycle begins with the last phase of an unhappy experience of love. The lover has come to realize the worthlessness of his beloved and knows at last that the love, which was the greatest experience of his life, has been squandered on one who was incapable of appreciating the unique gift of true love and faith. The girl had playfully accepted her lover's pledge and then without any compunction had broken his heart. He struggles to escape from his devotion to her. He tries to leave the surroundings where he has been so deeply wounded and betrayed. This cycle—through twenty-four songs—leads step by step to utter dissolution.

GUTE NACHT

Imagine that you are this man who is on the verge of complete disintegration. It is a cold winter night. A clear moon illuminates the snow-covered landscape with its cold white light. You have decided to leave during the night—for if you left in daylight, you might see her, from whom you are fleeing, and perhaps if you should see her again you would weaken and would not find the strength to go. But you can no longer bear the torture of being near her. You will lose your mind if you cannot escape from her.

You pass her house. You remember desperately how full of new hope and happiness the spring had seemed to you. Your love had seemed to bring fulfilment. The girl appeared to be devoted to you. Her mother had not opposed your marriage. Now the whole world has changed for you.

Begin the song with great bitterness. In the first lines you should convey the personality of this lonely and desperate man. Your voice, your words, are filled with scorn as you sing— 'Das Mädchen sprach von Liebe, die Mutter gar von Eh' . . .' Change to an expression of grief with 'Nun ist die Welt so trübe'.

The third verse has a slightly quickened tempo. 'Lass' irre Hunde heulen' should be sung with a kind of desperate contempt. 'Die Liebe liebt das Wandern' should convey suppressed scorn. Sing it *piano* and emphasize the consonants sharply. Give a very slight *crescendo* to: 'Von Einem zu dem Ander'n, Gott hat sie so gemacht'. Perhaps in one of the sad quarrels which were the prelude to the end of all your happiness she has said to you—'What do you expect? I cannot love you forever. God made life that way, you cannot blame me . . .' and now again he recalls her flippant answer to his pleading. (The interludes between verses should always be treated as if you were singing them yourself. Your facial expression must reflect the music as if it were floating from your whole being. The listener must have the impression that the cycle is just being created at this moment—that it is *you* who are writing the poems, *you* who are composing the music . . . Re-creation means: created anew.)

Your face should have an expression of deep sorrow as you

begin the last verse. Prepare for it. Look downward during the interlude and then when the key changes slowly raise your head and gaze before you. Imagine that you are passing her home, that you are passing the window behind which she is sleeping, oblivious to your grief and misery. You walk softly lest you disturb her carefree slumber. This last verse can quite rightly and effectively be sung with deep bitterness but I always sang it with the utmost tenderness, delicacy and subtlety. In this cycle there is so much opportunity for outbursts of bitterness and desperation that from the standpoint of building up the cycle I think it is better to sing this verse very *piano*. It is as if you do not want to touch the wound in your heart by speaking roughly to your beloved even in your thoughts. Sing 'sacht, sacht die Türe zu . . .' with a breathy *piano*. End with an expression of infinite pain: 'an dich hab' ich gedacht'—especially in the repetition—as if you were saying: 'You cannot know how I thought of you—leaving you . . . You do not care. You only think of me with indifference. But my thoughts are so tender, they float through your window to lie like roses at your feet . . . But you do not care . . .'

DIE WETTERFAHNE

You have left the house of your beloved. You have left her village. But you have no thought of where you are going or what you want to do. You want only to forget, but there is no road which leads to oblivion and peace. One who is possessed will always try to escape from that which possesses him. But it is in vain that you try to escape, for you are possessed by love and this love will not set you free. It holds you bound relentlessly to the one place. . . .

A grey and stormy morning finds you again at the very spot which you are seeking to avoid. Staring at her house with burning eyes, you subconsciously follow the weather-vane as it veers about in the wind.

In the prelude is the violence of the wind, but the violence of your own thoughts is also there. You have lived through so much agony, your thoughts are confused. It seems as if the vane, rattling and squeaking as it whirls, scorns you, scorns the innocent belief which you had in your beloved.

Begin this song with an expression of deep bitterness, of driving force. Avoid sliding—every note, every syllable must be clear cut and devoid of any weakness or sentimentality. Sing strongly until 'Ein treues Frauenbild'. Then change to *piano*, as if you were telling a secret—'Oh, how terrible it is that our hearts can be so weak as to become the victims of changing moods and whims!' They flutter as if the wind were tossing them about, but secretly . . . softly.

You do not blame your beloved for leaving you to marry another man. You only blame her parents. It makes it easier to think that it was they who forced her to give you up. You blame their fickle hearts which are like toys in the cruel wind. Sing 'was fragen sie' with *crescendo* until you end in a desperate *forte* with 'eine reiche Braut'. The repetition is sung in the same way. Your facial expression should reflect the violence and desperate hopelessness which engulfs you so completely.

GEFROR'NE TRÄNEN

Wandering aimlessly along the icy streets and snowswept roads, you feel the tears upon your cheeks, frozen by the icy wind. The first *staccato* chords of the prelude are like heavy, weary, staggering steps, while the *decrescendo* (softly *ritenuto*) is the wakening awareness of reality.

Tears which you weep, without realizing it, become the conscious expression of your inner pain. Sing the beginning very *legato* and without expression, sing from out of utter emptiness, from a feeling of inner cold, as if your deep pain is submerged beneath the frozen crust of complete hopelessness.

In the short interlude after 'dass ich geweinet hab' your icy numbness changes. Bitterness wells within you. Sing with suppressed passion, with mounting dramatic expression until the end—'des ganzen Winter's Eis' which should be sung broadly. In the postlude you sink again into yourself, wandering on, lonely, aimlessly.

ERSTARRUNG

Your wandering has changed into flight. Flight from this terrible emptiness, flight from the aimlessness which yet drives you on. You have been shaken out of your lethargy by the cold wind which blows over the frozen fields. With the quickened tempo of the prelude, you must give the impression of being driven on. A slight bending forward may be helpful in giving this impression but the principal thing is and will always be: *feel* that you are driven on, *feel* the cold wind. If you can do this, your expression will be convincing. I must always repeat: *only that is convincing which is truly felt*.

The two phrases—'ich such' im Schnee vergebens nach ihrer Tritte Spur, wo sie an meinem Arme durchstrich die grüne Flur' should be sung *legato*. Your remembrance of that happy time is here stronger than any thought of the present. Sing these phrases touched by a soft glow of reminiscence, but at the same time with animation as if you were increasing your pace. Imagine that your steps take on increasing urgency as you hurry on, while your eyes, searching mechanically, sweep over the broad expanse of white snow. But your feeling is pervaded by the glow of memory: 'wo sie an meinem Arme durchstrich die grüne Flur.' So your singing here must be soft and *legato*.

In the next verse you return to reality, to passionate desire, desperate grief. Sing it with dramatic fire. Note the two *crescendi* at 'bis ich die Erde, die Erde seh'. Feel the passionate restraint in this. There is brooding insanity in this bitter restraint.

In the next verse go back to the sweet *pianissimo* of remembrance, a *pianissimo* which is, so to speak, moist with tears. Note the *sforzati* at 'Blumen' and 'erstorben', but sing them discreetly. Feel the colourless emptiness in the word 'blass'. Paint it with consonants and with a very light '*a*' as if you were using water colours. Sing *ritenuto* to the end of the verse.

The *crescendo* and *forte* is the transition to the more passionate expression of the next verses. 'Wenn meine Schmerzen schweigen, wer sagt mir dann von ihr?' Your grief for your lost beloved is now almost a joy, since it gives you a feeling of contact with her. Your heart seems dead but perhaps it may yet melt like the frozen brook, and the vision of your beloved which it holds may be borne away on the flowing water. Feel the self-torturing pain in these words, this poetic picture, this stormy melody.

At the end the song fades into *decrescendo* and *ritardando* as if you yourself are breaking down under the tormenting power of your imagination. Convey the impression of complete exhaustion. Do not forget the little *crescendo* and *decrescendo* at the last 'dahin'.

DER LINDENBAUM

You seem to be going around in a circle. You try to get far away but the vicinity in which your beloved lives draws you back like a magnet so that you seem only to wander around and around. So you find yourself back again at the old gate where you have so often sat in the shade of the old lime tree.

You pause in your restless wandering as you suddenly find yourself beside the well under the old tree. You have forgotten all about the winter and its cold. You have forgotten your grief. A quiet peace comes upon you, as if at last you are at home. The first verse should be sung with the greatest simplicity, with warmth, very *legato*.

Begin the second verse a little more excitedly. At 'vorbei in tiefer Nacht' darkness again falls upon you. Your need to continue in your wandering is like a sombre compulsion. Sing this sentence with this thought. Yet the lime tree holds you back. It holds you with a mysterious strength. Sing 'Da hab' ich noch im Dunkel die Augen zugemacht' *pianissimo* with an expression of surrender. Now the branches speak to you through their rustling: sing this full voice, as if the wind were swelling through the treetop. Sing 'komm' her zu mir Geselle' entreatingly. But no: you tear yourself away from your dreams, you will not listen to the tree as it calls you back. Sing with dramatic force, deeply moved: 'die kalten Winde', etc. Bring to a highly dramatic climax the last sentence: 'ich wendete mich nicht'. Make use of the consonants and sing with sharp accentuation, uttering the 'nicht' as if you were tearing yourself loose from hands which seek to hold you back. You must give the impression that you are tearing yourself away, never more, *no, never more* to return.

But the compelling song of the tree is more powerful than your strength of will. It comes to you in your dreams. Sing the last verse with a quieter melancholy and give the last words—'du fändest Ruhe dort'—an alluring *pianissimo*, full of mystery.

WASSERFLUT

The important thing here is to be able to bring to life passionate feeling within the framework of a very austere melody. The rhythm must never be broken. The vital connection with the musical phrase can never be sundered. The more rhythmically you sing, the more you will succeed in bringing out the austere character of the song. Sing very quietly and make a glowing *crescendo* at: 'durstig ein das heisse Weh'. Accentuate the consonants sharply and stress the triplets. Sing 'Wenn die Gräser sprossen wollen' very tenderly. Sing 'weht daher ein lauer Wind' with a broad sweep. Your phrasing must float like a breath of wind.

To give too many details or too much advice for this song might lead to destroying the greatness of its line. The interpretation here really needs no explanation.

AUF DEM FLUSSE

The beginning of this song is pervaded by an icy clarity. The prelude conveys the impression of heartbeats throbbing beneath the ice.

Sing the first verse as if you are lost in quiet contemplation, without much expression. It must be sung with exact rhythm and strict attention to the value of every note.

In the second verse 'In deine Decke grab' ich' your emotion overflows. Your facial expression is one of dreaming, your voice should be filled with deep warmth. At the end of the verse: 'windet sich ein zerbroch'ner Ring,' you are overcome by grief. (Emphasize the consonants in 'zerbroch'ner'.) The throbbing heart beneath the ice seems like your own heart—life flowing beneath a crust of numbness—flooding passion which threatens to burst through the icy surface. Sing the four repetitions of 'ob's wohl auch so reissend schwillt' each time with increased drama—with a swelling *crescendo*. End vigorously.

RÜCKBLICK

Again you are in flight, again you are trying to escape. Your wandering has led you back to the very place which you have wanted to avoid. You are drawn back irresistibly, but again you tear yourself away. You have hurried on through the old familiar streets. Everywhere you feel that you are scorned.

The prelude gives the feeling of storm and of senseless racing ahead. Begin with a suppressed but passionate *piano* and at each 'Eis und Schnee' and 'die Türme seh' sing a surging and stormy *crescendo*. Note the *sforzati* at 'Krähe' and 'Bäll'.' Sing this verse distinctly, almost *parlando*, and close with a *legato* at the last 'jedem Haus' which leads over into the more measured tempo of the second verse. Reflect in your voice the change of key, sing with a softly flowing *legato*, in a lovely warm *piano*. Paint with both word and tone: the little town, the feeling of spring, the murmuring brook, the lime tree. Sing the phrase: 'da war's gescheh'n um dich Gesell' with a strongly exhaled *pianissimo* as if with tears of remembrance of all the loveliness which you have lost.

Again the key changes and with it your voice quality. Again restlessness seizes you. Each time, from out of suppressed misery, rises the *crescendo* which leads into a *forte*: 'noch einmal rückwärts seh'n' and 'ihrem Hause stille steh'n'. In the repetitions both voice and tempo quieten down: sing *legato* and with a yearning expression. Do not exaggerate the repeated *sforzati* (zurücke, wanken). Sing them discreetly.

The last 'vor ihrem Hause stille steh'n' fades away in a veiled *piano*, strictly in *tempo*.

IRRLICHT

This song is like a short dramatic scene. Sing it as such. Give this song a very individual character. Colour your voice more darkly and sing with an heroic expression. Give the song a broad, strong swing as you would an aria. Begin very quietly with strong accentuation. Sing with exact rhythm and give each note its exact value. 'Jedes Leiden auch sein Grab' should be sung with great warmth of feeling.

You know that your end is not far distant and with it the end of all your grief.

RAST

Your weary steps (heard in the prelude) have led you to a place where you may rest.

You must convey the picture of the tired wanderer who, with complete indifference, feels himself driven on by the raging storm, wandering wherever the wind may drive him. Sing the *pianissimo* in 'der Rücken fühlte keine Last' with a kind of bitter pleasure, but in the next phrase: 'der Sturm half fort mich wehen', convey the power of the storm. This is not a power which comes from you, yourself. It is a power which is aiding you, which you must express. So be careful here: the feeling of your inner exhaustion must not be lost through the *forte* of this phrase. (Perhaps I may make this clearer by saying that the first sentence is like a deep inhaled breath—*piano*; the second like a released exhaled breath.)

Begin the second verse very quietly. Enunciate the consonants in 'So brennen meine Wunden' sharply. Notice the sudden *piano* after the *crescendo*: your wound is so painful it hurts you even to mention it.

'Auch du, mein Herz' is filled with bitterness, as if you were saying derisively: 'Generally you are so courageous. But now in the quiet of repose you feel within you the gnawing worm which will consume you'. Sing these lines very distinctly, with a brightly coloured quality, making the consonants pointed and sharp. Close with a broad and dramatic *forte*.

FRÜHLINGSTRAUM

You are lying in the house of a collier where you have found shelter. You cannot wander any further, you must be patient and gather some strength. You are alone, you awaken out of the half sleep of deep exhaustion. The prelude conveys the dreams which pass so entrancingly through your half waking thoughts.

The first verse should be sung with a quietly floating quality, as if you were still under the spell of your lovely dream. Then

53

with your awakening comes grey reality: it is dark and cold and ravens circle ominously about the roof.

You must feel within yourself this awakening to a barren and sombre reality. Sing with force and with a feeling of deep pain. But you are sick and exhausted, you do not have sufficient strength to face reality, so you sink back, forgetting your gloomy surroundings and your eyes are caught by the weirdly formed and incredibly beautiful flowers frosted upon the window pane. Sing this whole verse *pianissimo* and *legato*. And so, with a tone carried upon your breath and with a fading smile, you sink again into your dream.

Sing the verse: 'Ich träumte von Lieb' und Liebe' as you did the first one, with animation.

After your first dream you awakened to the grey reality of the *outer* world. But now your heart awakens to the reality of your *inner* loneliness. You are so bitterly alone. You think of your dream which can never become reality. But so long as you may still breathe, so long will burn within you a spark of hope, however unfounded it may be. The last verse must be sung with a feeling of the deepest depression, yet a warm surge of hopefulness floods through you at the words: 'noch schlägt das Herz mir warm'.

A melancholy self-derision flows through 'wann grünt ihr Blätter am Fenster?' The last sentence should be sung like a sigh which gradually fades away. You are again half sleeping, half dreaming.

EINSAMKEIT

You have summoned yourself from your utter exhaustion and have wandered on, but you are wretched and weary. There is within you only a complete emptiness, a quiet which is not peace, a resignation which is only the result of your exhaustion and in no sense recovery.

The first verse should be sung without expression to 'und ohne Gruss'. With the following *crescendo* you take hold of yourself, the force of your grief returns to you and even if it is only with the vigour of complaint, nevertheless your heart glows again.

DIE POST

The foolish heart will always hope, even when it knows that hope is futile. So when the mail coach arrives, you listen even though you have no reason to do so.

The rhythm of the horses hoofs, the gay call of the posthorn have awakened you from your sad dreams. Against your will, you go to the window, asking yourself—'What is the matter with my heart, why should it beat so violently?' Accent 'hat' in 'was *hat* es' and sing the repetition with a sudden *piano*. (Accent '*hat*' here also.) The silent bar before the next phrase is your own sad realization that it is foolish of you to expect a letter. Now you sing quickly and with resignation—'Die Post bringt keinen Brief für dich'. Give a slight *crescendo* to 'was drängst du denn so wunderlich' and play with the consonants in 'drängst'. There must be a delicate charm in the repetitions of 'Mein Herz, mein Herz?' Imagine that your heart is like a bird which is eager to spread its wings. There must be a soaring and a sweeping quality in your voice and it should have a very slight vibration. Then the repetition of 'Die Post bringt keinen Brief für dich' has more inner strength, and you sing it with a mounting *crescendo*.

During the interlude you listen to the posthorn and at the same time you listen to your heart. You understand this restless beating, you understand the never-ceasing voice of your memories. Sing 'nun ja, die Post kommt aus der Stadt' softly and give a *crescendo* of painful memory to 'wo ich ein liebes Liebchen hatt' . . .' There is again a silent bar. Here it is your question to yourself—'but why am I so foolish? I know there is nothing for me to expect and yet I feel this burning longing. Oh I know, I understand: the coach comes from her town, perhaps they know how she is . . . Perhaps they know of what she is thinking . . . Oh my heart, my heart—do not fly away like a bird. Be still, my heart.' End the song stormily and with a broad *forte*. Breathe very shortly and quickly before the last 'mein Herz' and sing it as if it were a challenging call.

DER GREISE KOPF

This song, like 'Irrlicht' is to be sung as a dramatic scene. Begin it with grandeur—in a broad line, and enunciate clearly. There is a sharply accentuated *crescendo* at 'dass mir's vor meiner Jugend graut.' (Be very careful to give the exact value to each note.) Make a *sforzato* at 'graut'.

The next phrase—'wie weit noch bis zur Bahre'—should be like a soft, long-drawn sigh.

Begin the second verse in the same way as the first, broadly and with grandeur, but sing it more softly, as if you were thinking while you are singing—'can this really be possible? How can this happen to others but not to me?' End the song with intense feeling. Accentuate sharply each syllable and consonant.

DIE KRÄHE

Imagine this situation: for a long time a black crow has been circling about you. It has seemed like a dark and evil shadow about your head. Feel the uncanny atmosphere which surrounds you and pervades your being.

Sing the first verse as if you were inwardly numb, without any feeling. Your steadily flowing voice is filled with bitterness: 'Meinst wohl, bald als Beute hier.'

Exhausted, resigned, surrendering, you sing 'nun es wird nicht weit mehr geh'n' and your bitter despair over the ruining of your life bursts out in the final sentençe: 'Treue bis zum Grabe.'

The greater restraint with which the beginning of this song is sung, the more effective will be the wild outbreak at the end.

LETZTE HOFFNUNG

The *staccati* which begin in the prelude and continue to the end of this song are leaves falling in the autumn wind.

Do not *sing staccato*. Sing steadily as if with held breath. There is a light *ritenuto* at 'oftmals in Gedanken steh'n'.

The restrained anxiety with which you look up at the leaf,

as if your fate would be determined by whether it stayed or blew away, has in it a trace of insanity. So you should sing with a rather unnatural stiffness. Notice the *crescendo* and *decrescendo* at 'Ach und fällt das Blatt zu Boden'. Don't sing this *too* forcefully. It should be a kind of tone painting—a falling leaf blown about by the wind. This phrase must lead over into the insane whisper of 'fällt mit ihm die Hoffnung ab'. 'Fall' ich selber mit zu Boden' should be sung with great force (although the musical notations are the same as in the previous phrase) as if you are really breaking down. Then change your timbre and sing with deep emotion with a full dark tone: 'wein', wein' auf meiner Hoffnung Grab.'

These last phrases should have a broad sweeping grandeur and should pour out like the tone of a 'cello.

IM DORFE

Your restless wandering has led you to a sleeping town. The dogs bark, chains rattle. Unrest, beginning in the prelude, runs through the whole song up to 'ist alles zerflossen'. Sing this a little scornfully as if you were comforting yourself by saying: 'These people live in harmony together and share all that is good or bad. It is only I who am lonely and alone . . . But everything is transitory, even joy and sorrow—why should I envy them?' And yet your heart beats, warning you secretly. Certainly there is nothing which is not transitory, but these people, whom you do not know, have enjoyed what was denied you. And they will always find again their dreams of happiness—and hope, and hope . . . Sing these phrases with an expression of longing, giving your voice a bright and silvery quality. You are playing here with the dreams which other people experience and long for, you are singing of something floating and intangible. Give the words a light floating quality. With the passing of your dreams, reality again returns. You are driven away by the barking of the dogs who, mistrusting the unknown wanderer, surround you.

Sing with great bitterness and with a broad line until the end. Give the impression that you turn away, slowly wandering on, engulfed by the darkness of the night.

DER STÜRMISCHE MORGEN

Dawn, red like fire, has broken through the windswept clouds. The cold wind has aroused you. Once again you feel the will to fight. You would like to fight against your own weakness, your own self destruction.

The short prelude gives the setting for your stormy beginning.

Plunge, so to speak, into this very stirring melody, singing with vigorous accents. Your whole being is filled with animation, your eyes sparkle, you stand erect and defiant. You see your own heart in the image of the world ravaged by storm, it is cold and numb like winter itself. But at this moment it does not make you sad. As if in exultant madness, you feel yourself one with the uproar of nature. These strange, rather touching alternations between deepest depression and a surging will to live hold nothing surprising to the psychologist: on the contrary it is a well recognized symptom of mental illness.

The following song 'Täuschung' is the bridge which leads back from this state of inner exhilaration to the sombre urge towards self-destruction.

TÄUSCHUNG

The friendly, dance-like melody of the accompaniment is the confusing shimmer of the Will o' the Wisp which you are pursuing. Sing with an expression of mystery, as if you are under the spell of a power which you must obey. When you sing: 'und seh's ihm an, dass es verlockt den Wandersmann' make it obvious through your facial expression that you are *consciously* following the Will o' the Wisp. (It will help if you open your eyes wide, then half close them and sing with a light irony, as if you were saying: 'I know you, do not think for a moment that I do not realize that you are deceiving me.')

'Ach! wer wie ich so elend ist' is an outburst of deep pain. Sing this with a darkly-coloured timbre and then go over into a *piano* of restrained anguish. Emerging from the *pianissimo* you proceed broadly and heavily with 'die hinter Eis und Nacht und Graus'. Now you are again in your dream, the doors of a warm house seem to open before you and you find the spirit of your beloved. Sing these phrases softly as though you were dreaming, then suddenly you find reality again and sing with bitterness—'nur Täuschung ist für mich Gewinn.'

The melody of the Will o' the Wisp returns in the short postlude. Aware of what you are doing and so without any hope, you again follow it.

DER WEGWEISER

You have wandered here and there over the ice-covered countryside, but no others ever travelled along your road. You stand at a crossroads beside a signpost. With a tired glance, you look up at it and considering which road you would choose, you realize that you never choose the broad roads which others take, the roads which lead towards cities.

The prelude conveys your thoughts, introspective. The beginning of this song should be sung with a quiet thoughtful expression. From the repetition 'durch verschneite Felsenhöh'n' to the end of the first verse is sharply accentuated. The turbulent soaring of the music suggests the recollection of your conflicts and the dangerous and threatening icy road. But your thoughts only turn there for a moment; immediately they come back to yourself. The great 'warum' ('why') faces you and you raise your head singing with a very light, *pianissimo*, floating tone and in an almost childlike way: 'habe ja doch nichts begangen'.

Note the *sforzati* at 'törichtes' and 'in'. The 'in', however, should not be singled out, 'Wüsteneien' is the important word in this phrase. Bring together the strength of the music and the meaning of the sentence. Give a *sforzato* to each syllable. But you must do this very subtly. It seems almost dangerous to suggest this, for anything which is dependent upon the subtlest and most delicate feeling is very difficult to explain.

Begin the second verse in the same way as you did the first, lost in thought. At 'und ich wandre sonder Massen' you are overcome by restlessness. This should be sung *crescendo* with driving emotion. After the last 'suche Ruh' ' open your eyes wide here for you realize that there is only one thing which can bring you rest and peace: Death. Sing with a whispered *piano*, your eyes fixed rigidly upon some distant point, 'Einen Weiser seh' ich stehen unverrückt vor meinem Blick'. Then go over into a great *crescendo* with 'eine Strasse muss ich gehen . . .' as this realization closes upon you inescapably. In the repetition the *crescendo* does not again reach a *forte* climax.

The song ends with a feeling of quiet surrender. Hold the last 'zurück' as long as possible, letting it fade away gradually.

DAS WIRTSHAUS

In the prelude, your wandering steps halt before a gate. Looking up you realize that your way has led you to the entrance of a cemetery. With a gesture of finality you open the gate.

Whenever I hear this beautiful music, I see before me a little woodland cemetery in a German village, to which I used to go every year in days long gone by, to visit a cherished grave. Over the gate of this sanctuary, long forgotten by the world about it, was written in simple black letters on old and weatherbeaten wood—'Here dwells the peace which the world does not give.'

It is with this feeling that you must now (in your imagination) enter the cemetery.

Sing with great earnestness and a feeling of deep solemnity from the beginning to 'in's kühle Wirtshaus ein'. Be careful to avoid any inexactness here, do not make any *portamenti*, do not 'scoop'. The more purely, the more clearly and the less sentimentally you sing here, the nearer will you approach the ideal. This music is too uplifted, too heavenly beautiful, to be reproduced without the utmost reverence.

Bring out as much as is possible without exaggeration, the *ü* in 'müde Wanderer' and 'kühle Wirtshaus'. Feel the painting of tone in these words.

The next sentence, 'Sind denn in diesem Hause', should be sung with a veiled *pianissimo*. 'Bin matt zum Niedersinken' is like a sigh. Emphasize the word 'matt', but do it without any force. You can, if you do it with the greatest care, make an almost unnoticeable *portamento* at 'zum Niedersinken', but I am almost afraid to mention this, for it is dangerous advice. It can only be done with the very acme of subtlety. 'Bin tötlich schwer verletzt' is hardly more than breathed, it must be very restrained, sung, so to speak, with a fading heartbeat.

In the short interlude your eyes become alive, a shadow crosses your face. Colour your voice darkly. You tremble with pain: 'du unbarmherz'ge Schenke, doch weisest du mich ab?' and the next sentence 'Nun weiter denn . . .' is to be sung with the deepest resignation. Your voice becomes empty, light, colourless. The next words 'nur weiter' should have a delicate *crescendo* but one lacking in any force, as if with a sigh of resignation. The last bar is *ritardando*. Sing each syllable distinctly giving the impression of tired feet which wander on.

In the postlude you turn away and again wander on, purposeless, without any goal.

DER MUT

Once again you pull yourself together, once again you find the power of defiance. Life has closed for you the door to happiness. Death has refused you. What can be left for you? Yet once again your heart quickens, rebellious, ready to fight.

Your bearing should express the change which has come over you: you stand very erect, as if you were facing the fate which has so senselessly destroyed you.

Even in the first verse a great differentiation must be made: you cannot sing 'wenn mein Herz im Busen spricht' with the same force of tone and certainly not with the same expression with which you sing 'sing' ich hell und munter'. Your heart speaks to you in sombre tones, secretly, whispering. So you must sing *piano*, with a sorrowful expression. Then sing 'sing ich hell und munter' *forte*.

The same applies to the next phrases: 'Höre nicht, was es mir sagt' is secret, with suppressed fear, *piano*. 'Habe keine Ohren' is loud, accentuated, shrill. The following two phrases are again to be done in the same way.

The last verse is strongly rhythmical, loud, bold, challenging. It is as if one who is afraid of himself, whistles to drown his fear.

DIE NEBENSONNEN

But this moment of surging energy was only a deceptive one. Now you have sunk into further depths of melancholy. You can no longer struggle with either the world or yourself. Your

61

thoughts seem clouded and confused. Soon you will be lost in darkness and consumed by a horror which is worse than death.

I have often been asked what is meant by the three suns. This is a matter of opinion of which there are several. One might say: it is a foggy evening and the setting sun, penetrating through the fog in a strange mirage, gives the illusion of three suns.

A great musician takes the convincing view that by these three suns is meant: faith, hope and love. Faith in the beloved, in any kindly fate, has passed. Hope is dead. Only love remains and will not die. If only it would also die! Only in a complete inner emptiness can lie release. Much as I value this moving interpretation, I cannot entirely accept it for my own. Why should we search for a logical explanation? The man who wanders so tragically through this cycle, until spiritual dissolution engulfs him, thinks and feels with the soul of one who is ill. It does not seem strange to me that he sees before him the illusion of three suns. If you create the inner vision of three suns in your feeling, they are there *for you*—and, with you, for your audience.

The restrained prelude is your glance as it falls upon something strange and wonderful: from out of your sombre thoughts you see the shimmering suns. Sing this simple flowing melody in a mysterious, floating, light *piano*. Be rigid, as if you were staring at something, be restrained as if under the enchantment of some spell. You must prepare in this song for the last song, which follows it. Disintegration through self destruction is your melancholy fate. Prepare for this. This is the only way in which I can explain it: sing 'Die Nebensonnen' *uncannily*. Your audience must experience the same cold shiver which you feel. The *forte* which develops with a *crescendo* is very difficult to sing ('Und sie auch standen da so stier').

The three suns are there before you like a wall, tremendous, shining over you with cold splendour. Retain the same rigid, uncanny, motionless bearing (in voice, carriage, facial expression) up to 'doch in's Angesicht'. Now take the *crescendo* to the next phrase with your whole being: a wave of pain floods through you. You think of the two eyes of your beloved which once lighted your way. 'Ach neulich hatt' ich auch wohl drei, nun sind hinab die besten zwei . . .'

Beside the sun in the heavens shone the eyes of your beloved, which were like suns to you, but you have lost them, in darkness they have been extinguished for you. Sing this phrase veiled in tears, repressed, softly. Your eyes, which have been closed, open again in the short interlude and numbness comes back into your face.

End the song with the same lifeless expression of uncanny rigidity with which you began it.

DER LEIERMANN

In this song the greatest *lack* of expression is the acme of expression. Stand very stiffly, with an expression of absolute emptiness, your eyes half closed. Words fall from your lips in uniformly light tones, without any accents.

You have been repudiated by both life and death. Senselessly you sway along the road without either goal or purpose. Madness which has followed you along your way has spun its inescapable web about you, impelling you to become the companion of the poor old man, who, deluded and deranged, grinds away on his organ, amidst ice and snow, without any reason, for no one.

Bursting out in suppressed derision at yourself, you call to him: 'Will you not turn your organ to my songs?'

With a slight *crescendo*, you stagger towards the old man, the poor old fool, at whom dogs bark and whom human beings avoid. Darkness has fallen round about you. Darkness engulfs you. You are lost in nothingness, submerged in emptiness. . . .

SCHWANENGESANG

FRANZ SCHUBERT

Schwanengesang is the last group of Schubert's songs, all written in 1828, the year of his death. The title was not Schubert's, but was given to the group by his publisher, Haslinger.

Of the fourteen songs which comprise *Schwanengesang*, the first seven are to poems by *Ludwig Rellstab*, born 1799 in Berlin, died 1860, who is remembered today virtually through Schubert's settings alone. The next six are to poems by the great *Heinrich Heine* (1789–1856). And the final—and last of all Schubert's songs—'Die Taubenpost', is to a poem by *J. G. Seidl*, otherwise forgotten except as the author of the Austrian Imperial hymn.

LIEBESBOTSCHAFT
(*Rellstab*)

Through the whole song floats the soft music of the rustling brook. It is a friendly and gentle song without any dramatic ambition. You ask the brook to be your messenger—and always between your messages there are one and a half bars of accompanying music. You want the brook to carry your love to the maiden of whom you think so much. In your imagination you see her lovely garden of which she takes such care and you ask the brook to send its refreshing water to the plants and to the red roses.

The first verse ends and you have two full bars of rushing music before you start the second verse. You tell the brook that perhaps she may be sad, thinking of you, because you are so far away. So it shall console her and tell her that you will be home very soon. After three and a half bars, you continue very *pianissimo*: 'Neigt sich die Sonne mit rötlichem Schein, wiege das Liebchen in Schlummer ein', begging the brook to sing a soothing lullaby and to whisper dreams of love into her ear. The repetition of these last words is drawn out, and the song ends with the *diminuendo* of the accompaniment.

KRIEGERS AHNUNG
(*Rellstab*)

The music depicts with heavy but rather subdued chords the loneliness of the battlefield at night. All is quiet. There is a menacing stillness around you. Your comrades are asleep, but you are awake and your heart is heavy with fear and with longing. Here there is a strong *crescendo*, so that by the words 'so heiss' you reach the climax and drop down to a *mezzoforte* at the repetition. You remember now how happy you have been at home, sleeping in the arms of your beloved wife, your room lit by the friendly fire of the stove. The music here changes to a softly moving accompaniment.

Then very *pianissimo* and trembling: 'Hier, wo der Flammen düst'rer Schein ach, nur auf Waffen spielt'. You feel so totally alone and forgotten that tears run down your face. Each time the accompaniment has a strong *crescendo* and *decrescendo*. You know that you cannot go on if you lose your faith and with it your consolation, and you say to yourself: 'Herz, dass der Trost dich nicht verlässt, es ruft noch manche Schlacht'. The music becomes agitated and restless and when it dies down into *pianissimo*, it is only to express your dark premonition that soon you too will sleep, and with great emotion you say farewell to your beloved. All this is *pianissimo*. But the earlier mood returns as you sing: 'May this consolation never leave me, because many more battles will be fought', and you repeat your sad farewell to your beloved: 'Herzliebste, gute Nacht....'

The last *pianissimo* chords, dark and unearthly, seem to say that your sleep will indeed be an eternal one.

FRÜHLINGSSEHNSUCHT
(*Rellstab*)

This song starts with a rapid movement which runs through the whole three verses. The longing for spring is expressed with joyful expectation. Even the sense of sadness is described in the same quick tempo; only the question, 'und du?' has a *ritardando*. But this sadness is something which can be turned to happiness, and you hope it will be so one day; and this hope is mirrored throughout the song and holds you fast from the dark abyss. The last words, 'nur du, nur du!', are *fortissimo* and must be sung with a wonderful feeling of expectation and joy.

STÄNDCHEN
(*Rellstab*)

This Lied has almost become a folk song. I have heard it sung full *forte* throughout. But never forget that it is a serenade, something which has to be sung intimately and, of course, mostly *pianissimo*. You are standing beneath the window of your beloved and want to entice her away from her chamber, out into the garden. So you sing seductively and with great tenderness: 'Leise flehen meine Lieder durch die Nacht zu dir'. The guitar accompanies your pleading. You talk of the nightingale who would understand your longing because it is the messenger of love, and who begs her to hear you and to do as you ask. Nobody will know that you entered the garden; there is no one who would tell those who do not want her to follow you; she will be quite safe with you here in the garden. Then, in the last verse, you grow more urgent. You are no longer cautious and you sing with a sweeping *forte*: 'Lass' auch dir die Brust bewegen, Liebchen, höre mich!' The thought that she may come to you overwhelms you, and you close the song with a whispered sigh: 'Come and make me happy!'

The sound of the guitar continues, fading away into *pianissimo*.

AUFENTHALT
(*Rellstab*)

The music of the prelude describes the storm. There is a strong *crescendo* (from your *mezzoforte*) to *fortissimo*. Imagine yourself standing quite alone in the storm-ravaged forest. You feel at home here, your heart is agitated by an inner storm and tears are streaming down your face. When you sing: 'Wie sich die Welle an Welle reiht', sing it always with a gliding motion from word to word. With the interlude comes a sense of colour, and you start *piano* and very *legato*: 'Hoch in den Kronen wogend sich's regt, so unaufhörlich mein Herze schlägt'. In the repetition of these sentences, however, you sing *forte*, but do not forget the sweeping *legato* which seems to imitate the movement of the waves. You compare your own state of mind with the eternal, immovable rocks. And the short interlude brings you back to the phrases of the beginning: 'Rauschender Strom, brausender Wald, starrender Fels mein Aufenthalt'. After the last *fortissimo* ('starrender Fels') you sing *ritardando* and *diminuendo* till the end.

Be careful to sing this ending very *legato* and with a softer tone than you have used before. The postlude dies away—and in your imagination you see yourself standing in the midst of the storm which has brought you some measure of solace, even if you really do not feel it and acknowledge it yourself.

IN DER FERNE
(*Rellstab*)

'Woe to the fugitive, the wanderer from world to world!'
The words are full of menace. So too the prelude itself expresses
your feelings of warning and dread; first a strong chord,
followed by a broadly phrased question, and the piano music
fades into *pianissimo* before you start singing. Those who leave
their friends, those who forget their homeland, those who hate
the house of their fathers can never be happy in life. The interlude repeats the warning chords. In your inner heart you know
more than you are prepared to admit if you belong to those
wanderers, for you say: 'Herze, das sehnende Auge, das
tränende Sehnsucht nie endende',—and you realize that you
will be a 'hoffnungslos Sinkender'. Your voice, too, sinks into
the depths of despair. The interlude repeats the warning call of
the beginning.

The tempo becomes a little more agitated and the accompaniment soars with your singing voice like a fountain of tears.
At last you say why you are a fugitive, unmindful of your home
and friends: 'Die mir das Herze brach'—*she*, the one who has
been the cause of your unhappiness. *She* it was who broke your
heart and destroyed your life, *she* who made you flee from all
that you have loved. And your last outburst is a bitter accusa-
tion of the one who has made a fugitive of you. The song ends
with a strong *fortissimo*, like a cry of agony.

ABSCHIED
(*Rellstab*)

The sound of horse's hooves echoes throughout the song. It
is a happy farewell with no regrets. You say goodbye to the
town which you have loved so much, to all the streets through
which you have passed so many times. No one has ever seen
you sad, so your farewell, also, should be light-hearted and gay.
You say good-bye to the lovely gardens, the shimmering river.
Never did you sing a sad song, so, too, at the moment of farewell it will be a gay one. Goodbye to the friendly girls. You
looked at them smilingly and turned around, but not once did

your horse stop trotting. Now, far from the city illuminated by the setting sun you hesitate, and with you the piano music dies down to *pianissimo*. There is a window where you have often looked up, because the girl who lives behind this window meant more to you than you want to admit. Now, at the hour of farewell, you tell the stars that their shining light could never be a substitute for the bright reflection of this unique window. The stars will follow you; you must leave. It will not help you that the whole world lies before you under these shimmering stars. So your song ends on a sad note, even if you did not want it so. But you could not keep up the false gaiety, and the sound of your horse's hooves is now sad and forlorn, and fades away as you disappear in the distance.

DER ATLAS
(*Heine*)

This is not the Atlas of the myth, the man who revolted against the Gods and as punishment was made to carry the whole heaven on his shoulders. This man, who suffers as Atlas suffered, is a human being. It could be you or I who feels the burden of the whole world on our shoulders. The first chords seem to illustrate the suffocating weight of this burden. These chords have an overwhelming strength which dominates the whole song. The piano accompaniment trembles and rages, and the voice echoes this feeling of total despair: 'Ich unglücksel' ger Atlas! Eine Welt, die ganze Welt der Schmerzen muss ich tragen!' It is a weight of suffering past all bearing. But then the music becomes quieter at the words: 'du stolzes Herz, du hast es ja gewollt'. Yes, this is what you wanted. Your wish is fulfilled: 'Now you are miserable'. With these words a violent *fortissimo* leads back to a repetition of the opening phrases and ends with the bitter cry: 'Die ganze Welt der Schmerzen muss ich tragen!'

IHR BILD
(*Heine*)

It is most important here that you sing *legato*. The phrases are long-drawn and have to be sung very softly, almost as if in a dream. The song begins with two soft chords and your voice must have the same quality of a gentle *pianissimo*. Observe the two points at 'Starrt' ihr Bildnis an'. It seems to me that this rather surprising bar has the effect of a heart which suddenly stops beating. The piano music repeats the same phrase. Then your voice has a soft *legato* at the words: 'Und das geliebte Antlitz heimlich zu leben begann'. You looked so fixedly at the picture of your beloved that it seemed to you as if it came alive. You saw the smile which you had loved so much, you saw the tears in her beautiful eyes. The music stops as if in awe. Then you say that your tears, too, begin to fall; and now, after some dark chords in the piano accompaniment, you sing in a full *crescendo*: 'Und ach, ich kann es nicht glauben, dass ich dich verloren hab' '. The dream is over, the bitter reality breaks through in these despairing words. The postlude ends in a strong *forte*.

DAS FISCHERMÄDCHEN
(*Heine*)

The prelude sets the dancing rhythm which runs through this gay song. Imagine yourself sitting by the seashore and looking out to sea, where the little boat of the daughter of one of the fishermen is coming towards you. She fascinates you and you call to her gaily: 'Du schönes Fischermädchen, treibe den Kahn an's Land'. You want her to come to you, to sit by your side and let you caress her hand. You listen for her reply. Perhaps she does not answer. Or *did* she hear you? Perhaps she did. Perhaps she sits down beside you; but she seems a little frightened, so you say: 'Leg' an mein Herz dein Köpfchen und fürchte dich nicht so sehr'. You see that she is afraid and I cannot blame her. I think you were, perhaps, a little bold in your approach. But you tell her that she seems to be without fear of the wild waves. Why then should she be afraid of you? The dancing rhythm continues in the piano music, but in a very light *piano*.

You tell the girl that your heart is like the sea with which she is so familiar, and that it also has some precious pearls in its depths. I do not know how the fisherman's lovely maiden reacted to this story. The postlude does not tell us, but it dies away in a soft *pianissimo* which may mean that she did not exactly refuse you. . . .

DIE STADT
(*Heine*)

The long prelude has a melancholy air. From a *pianissimo* start it leads to a *decrescendo*. A soft wind passes over the surface of the sea, touching it with gentle wings. But when your voice starts to sing the melody the piano goes along with you. Be careful to observe the dots; be *very* accurate. Sing softly! The second verse pictures the swaying wind which ruffles the grey water, and your helmsman is sad like you yourself. The wind vanishes in a *pianissimo* which is scarcely audible. Then you sing in a strong *forte*: 'Die Sonne hebt sich noch einmal leuchtend vom Boden empor'. The sun appears from behind the clouds and as it sinks below the horizon, it lights the town where you have lost all that you had loved most. The interlude again floats away on the wings of the wind.

AM MEER
(*Heine*)

The first two bars already strike a dark and sombre note. At the beginning you should sing *molto legato* with a swaying *pianissimo*: 'Das Meer erglänzte weit hinaus im letzten Abendscheine'. But clouds are already rolling towards the shore, as sadness had come into your life after a short moment of happiness. You sit there silent and quite alone. Perhaps it is for a last farewell that you have met here secretly. Both of you feel the utter hopelessness of your love, and therefore the wide horizon seems to be empty for you. The fog lies like a shroud upon the sea, the waves roll in with the rising tide, the gull is flying anxiously to and fro. You turn your face towards your beloved, seeking some consolation in her quiet eyes, but instead you see the tears falling upon her hand. Your strength deserts you: you break down, and falling on your knees, you drink the bitter tears from her hand.

From this moment you are lost. It is as if these tears have poisoned your heart and your whole being. You feel that you are doomed. The accompanying music foreshadows the end, and trembles as, trembling too, you sing: 'Die Seele stirbt vor Sehnen'. The two chords which close the song are *pianissimo* and *ppp*—like a dying sigh.

DER DOPPELGÄNGER
(*Heine*)

It is very important for you to visualize clearly the background of this dark, mysterious Lied, with its ballad-like quality. Feel the mystery of the still, moonlit night. Feel the silence all around you. See the ghostly shadows of the houses and the motionless trees. See yourself standing there as if transfixed, utterly alone, your pale face raised towards the windows behind which your beloved once lived.

The first four bars of the prelude paint more vividly and more nobly than any words the atmosphere of this night so charged with mystery. There is brooding tragedy in the sombre *pianissimo* chords. I can never hear them without shivering. Sing with the utmost *legato*, with a darkly coloured timbre, *pianissimo* and without any trace of sentimentality. Avoid any slurring (do not slide or scoop.) Change your timbre at 'In diesem Hause wohnte mein Schatz'. You tremble with the pain of your suppressed longing. Your voice is now a little more brightly coloured, your face has an expression of grief. You see clearly before you the forsaken house as it stands in the brilliant moonlight, its windows like black holes staring at you with empty eyes. Sing 'Sie hat schon längst die Stadt verlassen' with bitterness and with a tormented expression; and as if with astonishment sing 'doch steht noch das Haus'. (Have you ever in your experience lived through a sorrow so great that you simply could not realize that the world around you has gone on as if nothing had happened? When one loses a loved one forever, it is hard to understand that nothing else has changed, that the world is the same old world.) Your voice should convey this feeling of sadness and disbelief, when you sing 'doch steht noch das Haus'.

It is as if your mind were confused. Perhaps you see your reflection like a shadow on the moonlit window-panes, perhaps in your bewilderment you create a phantom image of

yourself which stares at you from out of the darkness. Sing 'da
steht auch ein Mensch' in a veiled *pianissimo* as if paralysed
by your mounting horror. Develop the *crescendo* which leads
up to a *fff* ascending broadly to a climax. Sing 'mir graut
es' very distinctly but at the same time very *piano*, breathing audibly and with an inner trembling. The *crescendo* mounting to *fff* is a still further increase in volume beyond that of the
preceding phrase. If the power of your voice cannot be greater
than *fff*, you can still attain an increased effect of power
through your expression. Sing with a feeling of wild horror
'eigene Gestalt'. If I suggest that you should sing the phrases
that follow *gaspingly*, I do not mean this too literally. Never
forget that you must respect the limits imposed by the style of
Lieder singing. Try to find out how you would speak these
words if you were an actor. Recite them, and then transfer this
expression to the restricted frame of the song. Sing with great
bitterness, *crescendo*, mounting in both tempo and expression.
Note *exactly* every dot, sing with sharp accentuation and with
very distinct enunciation. Pause after the *ff* chord and do not
overlook the quarter rest before you begin to sing broadly and
forcefully and with dramatic power 'so manche Nacht'. Sing
a *subito pianissimo* at 'in alter Zeit'. It is as if you were saying to
yourself: it is so long, so very long I have suffered that I have
forgotten that I was ever happy. I do not dare to think how
long I have been in such despair. I am ashamed at my weakness which chains me to this scene of my unhappiness. All
these feelings flow together in the words 'in alter Zeit', flow in a
stirring *pianissimo*, and run like quiet tears over your face, which,
disconsolate and without hope, looks up at the white moon.

Remain so until the end of the postlude dies away.

DIE TAUBENPOST
(*Seidl*)

The melody which runs through this lovely song is very
even and without any great dynamic variation. You tell of the
faithful carrier pigeon which serves you untiringly by day and
by night. It flies to the house of your beloved and takes her
messages and brings them back to you. In the short interludes
you see the pigeon flying and are glad to follow it on its happy

and undisturbed flight. Sing *pianissimo*: 'Dort schaut sie zum Fenster heimlich hinein', and you feel as if you were with her in her room. When you sing 'Gibt meine Grüsse scherzend ab', sing this 'scherzend' slightly staccato. Then follow with a *crescendo*: 'Kein Briefchen brauch' ich zu schreiben mehr'. You send her a tear, a tear from the heart, a tear which did not hurt you very much, because you know that this tear will be treasured by your girl. You know also that the pigeon, your friendly messenger, will bring this tear to her and you are quite unable to reward it. If it can serve you, that is enough reward for this faithful pigeon. But now you have told enough about it without disclosing its name. It is something we all know only too well; it is: 'Die Sehnsucht'. It is yearning, desire, longing. All this is included in the word 'Sehnsucht'. But this song does not express a longing which is without hope. On the contrary this longing always finds its way to a heart which gives back in return the same love, the same longing.

DICHTERLIEBE

ROBERT SCHUMANN

Born 1810, at Zwickau in Saxony, died 1856 in a lunatic asylum at Enderich, near Bonn. *Dichterliebe* was composed in 1840, the year of the composer's marriage to Clara Wieck, truly an *annus mirabilis* which also included the cycle *Frauenliebe und -Leben* and the Eichendorff *Liederkreis*.

HEINRICH HEINE

Born 1789 in Düsseldorf, died 1856 in Paris. Cynical, bitter, witty, he was perhaps the profoundest and—with Goethe— the greatest German lyric poet of the nineteenth century. His distaste for all things German led him to self-imposed exile in Paris.

I *Im wunderschönen Monat Mai*

Be careful not to sing this song sentimentally. It is a young man who tells of his love; never forget this. What the young girl might perhaps express shyly and hesitantly becomes enthusiasm and glowing passion when expressed by this enamoured poet.

Submerge yourself in the flowing poetry of the prelude which has the quality of flowering branches swaying in the breezes of spring. Begin *piano* but rapturously. Sing 'Im wunderschönen Monat Mai' with an ecstatic expression—feel the wonder and beauty of spring, paint delightedly, as if you saw before you a garden filled with flowers.

Sing with a broad *crescendo* up to 'die Liebe aufgegangen'. This phrase is vocally very difficult. You can make the word 'aufgegangen' easier by not making the consonants too distinct. This advice seems to me rather a sin against the Holy Ghost of expression, but it is better here to choose the lesser of two evils: better here (as an *exception*, please!) to be indistinct rather than to struggle vocally and give the impression that you cannot master the phrase from the technical standpoint. Sing the syllable 'gen' in 'aufgegangen' very broadly, making the 'e' in 'gen' sound like the 'a' in 'gang'. Bring the dreaming delight of the first verse to a passionate exuberance in the second verse. Be careful to give each dotted note and each semiquaver its exact value. They take from the song all trace of sentimentality. And above all avoid any scooping or sliding.

II *Aus meinen Tränen spriessen*

The tears and sighs of which you sing here do not imply any grief. They are the sweet tears and trembling sighs of passionate desire. So begin with an ethereal and silvery quality of voice. Notice the musical difference in the second and fourth phrases. In the second phrase the notes are delicately tied, whereas in

79

the fourth phrase they are dotted. From this differentiation arises an absolutely enchanting effect of tone painting. The flowers seem to be crowded close together—a garden full, meadows full of flowers—motionless in the radiant sunlight. The chorus of nightingales on the other hand is passionately alive and sings sweetly from out of the bushes.

The next phrase, 'und wenn du mich lieb hast, Kindchen', sing brightly, joyously, tenderly. It is almost as if you were speaking to a child. Accent 'schenk' in 'schenk' ich dir die Blumen all'; sing it with a whimsical expression. And sing the ending 'und vor deinem Fenster soll klingen das Lied der Nachtigall' very *legato* and tenderly, as if in a dream.

III Die Rose, die Lilie, die Taube, die Sonne

Above all things, this song should never be sung as if it were a virtuoso piece. The tempo is not excessively fast and it is not a situation which calls for a display of your long breath. I have even heard singers who were determined to rattle through this song on one breath and who were infinitely proud of this virtuoso accomplishment. The tempo should be gay, not hasty. The quick flow of words is enchanting: happiness overflows in these ecstatic and amorous phrases—stammering confession, rapturous bliss. Do not sing in a straight line, sing in swinging phrases. Recite the poem in a rapid tempo, noting which words are the high points as you recite them and you will then find the same high points in the musical phrase. Sing 'sie selber, aller Liebe Wonne' very *legato*. Note the following *ritardando* which goes over into *a tempo* at 'Taube'. Breathe deeply before the final 'die Eine'. Sing it as if it were a sigh of delight.

IV Wenn ich in deine Augen seh

The bright sun which has shone upon your love is clouded: you now begin to see your beloved with clearer eyes, and in your inner being you realize that she does not match that ideal image which you have held in your heart. You are no longer free from suffering, for you are a victim of your love even though you know that your beloved is not worthy of it.

Begin this song from out of this inner realization. Begin with a sad smile, as if emerging from a dream. At 'doch wenn ich küsse deinen Mund' you are overcome by passion. Sing it broadly, flowing, as if transported. The following phrases should be sung with a veiled *piano* as if under a spell of enchantment.

'Doch wenn du sprichst "ich liebe dich" ' comes like a warning. You know it is not the truth. These are empty words. And your answer is bitter tears.

This song is very easy to build up if you clearly understand its logical construction: her look comforts, her kiss heals, her nearness is intoxicating—but her promise of love is false and so brings a painful awakening for you.

V *Ich will meine Seele tauchen*

Now you turn away from your grief and pain and seek peace in your loving thoughts. You search for words, for comparisons with which to express your love. No picture is beautiful enough, no word subtle enough, no comparison ethereal enough to convey the fullness of your devotion. This song should be filled with trembling emotion. Sing with a veiled *piano*, floating, unreal. Paint with consonants in 'Das Lied soll schauern und beben', lift out the *sch* and the *b*—'*sch*auern', '*b*eben', but do it without breaking the soft flow of the melody.

End the song with a broad surge at 'den sie mir einst gegeben' and sing the triplet broadly and distinctly in 'wunderbar süsser Stund'. Sing it with closed eyes and an expression of blissful rapture as you recall the happiest moment in this experience of love.

VI *Im Rhein, im heiligen Strome*

In the first phrases paint the description of the lovely old city of Cologne with a broad line. Be careful not to force on the *e* and *f*. The low position and the desire to sing with great breadth may be dangerous for you. However it is not necessary to force your tone in order to give strong *expression*: pronounce distinctly, lift out the principal word, sing with nobility, and you will be more expressive than if you sing merely loudly.

At 'Im Dom' your expression changes. Imagine that you

have often passed through the cathedral completely under the spell of the consecrated solemnity which embraced you as you felt the presence of God about you. And you are compelled again and again to stand before the lovely image of the Madonna whose serene beauty stirs your heart. Sing with a soft *legato*, in a veiled *piano* as if under a spell. Your eyes, looking into the distance, are (in your thoughts) uplifted to this picture. It is the most beautiful which you have ever seen. From out of the confusion which has beset you, you have looked up at it and it has seemed to shine upon you. Sing 'in meines Lebens Wildnis hat's freundlich hinein gestrahlt' like a prayer of thanksgiving. It is like a miraculous image for you and you tell of it with delight, as if it lived and were radiant within your heart: 'es schweben Blumen . . .' With astonishment you realize that this exalted face of the holy Virgin is like the beautiful face of your beloved. Sing with a smiling melancholy: 'die gleichen der Liebsten genau'. Hold this expression of tender melancholy until you feel the fateful heavy *crescendo* in the postlude; this is your realization that, while your beloved may *outwardly* resemble the holy picture, the likeness is only superficial. With the heavy and increasingly sombre music, you slowly bow your head as if to hide your grief-stricken face, overwhelmed by the depths of misery which the image of the holy Virgin, however pure and beautiful, could not lift from your soul.

VII *Ich grolle nicht*

Now, for the first time, you tell clearly how deeply you are aware of the true nature of your beloved. Make the situation clear to yourself, consider what has happened to cause you to sing as you now do. There must have been a disagreement between you. Hard words have been spoken, confessions made, which have destroyed every bond that had remained between you. She is 'forever lost' to you ('ewig verlor'nes Lieb')—so you say and so you feel. But she, who has wounded you so deeply, believes that with a friendly 'Don't be cross', she can make everything all right again. You look up; with a bitter smile, you reject her suggestion that you are only 'cross'. Sing 'ich grolle nicht' broadly, with bitterness and with pride.

Change the quality of your voice which has been dark and

flowing, at 'Wie du auch strahlst in Diamantenpracht'. Sing
with a bright tone, disparagingly and ironically, as if you were
saying: 'But don't think that I don't see through you! The
splendour with which you surround yourself is all on the outside—don't think that you can fool me, that you can make me
forget what you really are!' Sing broadly, with sad accentuation, 'das weiss ich längst'.

I have always sung the second verse *piano*. Turning away
from your beloved, still trembling from your outbreak of
bitterness, you now speak more to yourself. For the first time
you have told her that you have seen through her, perhaps for
the first time you have clearly admitted it to yourself. Now
completely absorbed by your own thoughts you repeat,
trembling, 'Ich grolle nicht'. Beginning this verse with a
restrained *piano* will also give a stronger effect in building up
the dramatic climax of the song.

Sing 'Ich sah dich ja im Traume' in a whispered *piano*, as one
would whisper when telling a shocking secret. Build up the
crescendo with grandeur until 'die dir am Herzen frisst', and be
careful that 'Herzen' is not emphasized to the extent of losing
its connection with the preceding words. Even this violent
outburst must not overstep the limits of tonal beauty. Sing the
following phrase—'ich sah, mein Lieb, wie sehr du elend bist'
—broadly, each syllable *sforzato*. These words, these notes are
like the blows of a hammer which destroys the picture of out-
ward splendour. The repetition of 'ich grolle nicht' should be
strong, with deep emotion, as if through tears.

VIII Und wüssten's die Blumen

Sing with increased tempo as if driven by an inner feeling
of unrest. Do not try to make something characteristically
different of the flowers, the nightingales, the stars. The torment
of your own heart is the important thing here. It runs through
the whole song in one single thread of grief. At 'sie alle können's
nicht wissen' sing *pianissimo*, as if you were saying to yourself—
whispering, explaining—'How could the world know how
deeply I am wounded?'

In the next phrase, 'Nur eine kennt meinen Schmerz', colour
your voice darkly and end with deep bitterness and with

strong accentuation, hurling out the last 'zerrissen mir das Herz'.

IX *Das ist ein Flöten und Geigen*

In this song, the wild tumult of the piano accompaniment is the real melody, the voice being interwoven with it. Imagine that you are standing there amid the welter of your thoughts, feelings, fantasies. You are a defenceless victim: your mind is confused, your strength paralysed; you are a sacrifice to the sorcery of your imagination.

Sing with an expression as if you are listening, as if under a spell. You stand very rigid, very erect, conscious of the tumult around you. Note the rhythm which is always repeated. Do not neglect this. It gives the song the strange, savage air of austerity which is necessary. Remain under the spell of your visions until the end of the postlude. Listen to it as it dies away, as you would to a distant sound.

X *Hör' ich das Liedchen klingen*

From out of the confusion and gloom you find your way back to the soft melancholy of memory. This song should be sung with soft and flowing tones but without any sentimentality. At 'es treibt mich ein dunkles Sehnen hinauf zur Waldeshöh'', colour your voice darkly. Sing this with a deep inner longing. Tie the two syllables of 'Sehnen' and also of 'höh' in a strong curve, dark and glowing. Change the tone quality to the softest light silvery quality at 'dort löst sich auf in Tränen . . .' End as if with tears. In the postlude the dreamy mood which has surrounded you like a consoling dream is transformed into this bitter realization: in reality, I am not released and freed, I shall be destroyed by this love which consumes me.

XI *Ein Jüngling liebt ein Mädchen*

It is easy to explain psychologically that a human being caught in the grief of a doomed passion may suddenly, and objectively, analyze this passion and strip it of its romantic aura. It is like a moment of sanity in a state of madness, like finding safety on an island in the midst of a threatening sea.

This escape from the love which threatens to engulf you demands an entirely different kind of interpretation. This song must stand out from the rest of the cycle in the same way the objective self-analysis stands out from the wreath of poetry.

I should like to suggest that you sing this song almost like a couplet, if it did not sound too revolutionary to say such a thing about a song by Schumann. A sharply accentuated *parlando* lifts this song out from the others. Sing it as if you were describing something quite objectively, as if you wanted to say: 'What ridiculous things happen in life!' When you sing 'Der Jüngling ist übel d'ran', do it with a bitter smile of self-scorn. At the end of the song you withdraw into yourself: the mask falls, your apparently gay objectivity vanishes, grief again engulfs you.

Scorn breaks out again in the postlude but in the final chords you return to a feeling of tragedy, to sombre darkness, and this provides the transition to the next song.

XII *Am leuchtenden Sommermorgen*

The sweetest of poetry follows this outbreak of realism. The flight into bitter laughter has failed, you are more than ever submerged in love and grief. Take up immediately with your whole body the melody of the accompaniment which has the fragile quality of falling dewdrops.

Sing very softly and ethereally. 'Es flüstern und sprechen die Blumen' must be whispered and 'ich aber wandle stumm' should be broad and tender, as if with a muted violin tone.

From the whispered *piano* of 'Es flüstern und sprechen die Blumen und schau'n mitleidig mich an' go over into a light, silvery veiled *pianissimo*. It is the flowers who speak, so you must sing with an unearthly, floating quality: 'Sei uns'rer Schwester nicht böse, du trauriger blasser Mann'.

Remain under the spell of this enchanting music until the postlude has faded away.

XIII *Ich hab' im Traum geweinet*

Begin with quiet sadness. Your voice, your whole being emerges from melancholy dreams. Sing the beginning of this

song with restrained feeling, as if you were not entirely
awakened to the reality of your grief. (Do not forget: you
repeat the same sentence three times. You must *build up*!) The
same mood, the same soft, sombre sadness lasts until the end of
the first verse—'floss noch von der Wange herab'.

Sing the second 'Ich hab' im Traum geweinet' with mounting expression, yet with restraint. 'Mir träumt', du verliessest
mich' is born of an inner shudder, from tormenting fear. The
following phrase, 'Ich wachte auf', should be sung with
increased power. It has become reality, a painful awakening
from the darkness of dreams, to the greyness of day. At 'noch
lange bitterlich' sing '*l*ange *bitt*erlich' with marked accentuation (the *l*, *b*, *tt* should be very distinct).

Now the accompaniment takes up your words and your
facial expression shows your growing passion. With wide open
eyes you listen to the piano melody which tells of the feeling in
your heart.

Your last 'Ich hab' im Traum geweinet' is, to be sure, *pianissimo* but it must nevertheless be filled with passion. Sing 'mir
träumte, du wärst mir noch gut' broadly and sadly. Now sing
the end of the song in an outburst of despair. Your last word—
'Tränenflut'—breaks off as if in a sob. Remain rigid with grief
until the final chords of the postlude fade away.

XIV *Allnächtlich im Traume seh ich dich*

Again it is a dream which moves you. (Notice how after the
one sudden outbreak of realistic self-scorn in 'Ein Jüngling liebt'
ein Mädchen', you turned away from reality: flowers spoke to
you, dark dreams oppressed you. Now again comes a dream
which is kindly and comforting and brings you solace.) Sing
the whole song as if you are breathless. You are excited, it is as
if you want to hold fast something which is passing by. Your
heart beats, your whole being is in confusion, but your joy is
fragile and unreal. Your voice must be tender, flowing, with
an inner animation and full of subtle joy. 'Und laut aufweinend
stürz' ich mich zu deinen süssen Füssen' is an outburst of
violent passion. Do not sing loudly, there is no *forte* tone in this
whole song, but sing with strong accentuation, with grandeur
and with fire.

Paint with your tone the delicate appearance of the beloved, for example: 'schüttelst, schüttelst das blonde Köpfchen'. Do not breathe after the second 'schüttelst', but hold the tension, while making a short break between the words. (This, more than breathing, gives the impression that your heart has stopped beating.) The *crescendo* in the next phrase is only a slight one— you cannot speak of pearly tear-drops in a *forte* tone.

Sing 'du sagst mir heimlich ein leises Wort' with increased expression but always *piano*. The vision of your beloved seems to come nearer to you, nearer, more loving, more intimate. She offers you your wreath and you take it in your hands, but with a shock you see that it is a cypress wreath plucked from the trees which grow in the cemetery. Sing 'ich wache auf' heavily, then with a sudden *crescendo* 'und der Strauss ist fort', and sing the last phrase, 'und's Wort hab' ich vergessen', very quickly, as if it were a whisper.

XV Aus alten Märchen winkt es

Dreams and fairy-tales seem the only refuge for you from the darkness of your day. After dreams which have shaken you, after dreams which have brought to you the lovely vision of your beloved, the gates of a wonderland, which is more than a dream, open before you: the land of fairy-tales. Retreating into loneliness, you let your thoughts wander through the gay enchanted gardens of the old fairy-tale which you remember from the days of your childhood.

Sing this song soaringly, in a lively tempo, with an expression of rapture. Your soul again has wings, as it used to have in that carefree time when passion had not yet darkened your life. Sing with inner joy, feeling yourself free since you have found the strength which has raised you above this ill-fated love. Begin with a tone full of mystery and sing in a beautiful, soaring curve: 'da singt es und da klingt es von einem Zauberland'. Return immediately to a *pianissimo* at 'wo bunte Blumen blühen'. Sing this very softly, with a silvery tone. At 'und grüne Bäume singen uralte Melodei'n' colour your voice more darkly and sing with a broad sweep. Feel the murmur of the forest, the swaying of the leafy branches in the summer breeze. It seems strange that the melody at 'und Nebelbilder steigen wohl aus der Erd' hervor' should seem so forceful, so strong and realistic. But in a fairy-tale, the wonders are reality! The cloud images contain nothing ghostly. They are dark and compact figures which dance their strange rounds before you. Will-o'-the-wisps, shining blue and red, flutter and shimmer about you. You are bewitched with astonishment and delight. Quicken the tempo, sing very distinctly, play with the consonants. Especially let the *r*'s roll in 'im irren, wirren Kreis'. The fairy world seems to become more and more real to you. Yet suddenly the realization dawns on you: it is all only a dream. It is the enchanted world of your longing, the old for-ever unattainable fairy world which lies far beyond all seas, behind all mountains. Sing broadly, with inner warmth, in a full flow of passionate desire from 'Ach, könnt' ich dorthin kommen' to 'doch kommt die Morgensonne'. A great, quiet sadness comes upon you as you end the song. A sad smile plays about your mouth as you see disappearing before you that which was nothing more than a mirage.

In the postlude, the dissolving fairy world seems to touch you yet again, like a pale shadow.

XVI *Die alten, bösen Lieder*

This final song is certainly more suited to a man than to a woman. If you, the woman singer, are to make it credible, you must sing with great power of expression rather than force of tone.

Imagine the situation: you have now passed through every stage of delight, disillusionment, bitterness. You have sought oblivion in nature, in dreams, in fantasies, which have led you away from the world of reality. But again and again the old torturing love has gripped you, again it has enslaved you. Now at last you decide to end this torment once and for all if you are not to be destroyed by it. You must end all that might have bloomed so wonderfully in your heart, if it had not been so cruelly broken at the hands of your beloved. The songs which you have sung in joy and sorrow must be silenced, the dreams which have tormented and comforted you must vanish.

Begin the song very erect, with great energy, sing broadly and forcefully. (Note the exact value of each note. Every dot is a valuable aid to expression.) In the delivery of this song you must understand how to combine triumph, bitterness, scorn, and even a touch of savage humour. You are now above pain, your fears are conquered, your sighs stilled. You have emptied your heart of every tender and vulnerable feeling. You have become master of yourself. The songs, the dreams, the tears have only made you unhappy. Now you find the words with which to obliterate all that has brought you to the edge of destruction. Sing in this way to 'gebürt ein grosses Grab'.

In the next phrase it is as if you suddenly stand still, as if you suddenly interrupt the grand gesture with which you had, so to speak, conducted the dramatic structure of this scene. You whisper—and something akin to madness sounds through this whispered question—'Wisst ihr, warum der Sarg wohl so gross und schwer mag sein?' Slide the word 'sein' up to the next phrase in a broad sweep: 'Ich senkt' auch meine Liebe und meinen Schmerz hinein'. Sing this broadly, painfully, through your tears. All your suffering, all your love, the whole blossoming world of your inner feeling pours out from you. Breathe before 'hinein' with a great and exalted finality. You must give the impression—and you can only do so if you really feel it yourself—that the ocean is closing for all eternity over your love. You have torn away from yourself and have buried all that you once felt. Now you are alone, engulfed in inner and outer emptiness.

In the postlude memory enfolds you. You listen to its melodies as to something long vanished. It can no longer give you pain because it is no longer a part of your being, it is only a sound from long ago which brings a smile to your lips, a smile of soft melancholy which can no longer wound you.

FRAUENLIEBE UND -LEBEN

ROBERT SCHUMANN

Frauenliebe und -Leben was composed in 1840, shortly before *Dichterliebe*.

ADALBERT VON CHAMISSO

Born 1781 at Castle Boncourt in Champagne, died 1838 in Berlin. A poet of sensitive, if sentimental, verse and best remembered for his romantic novel *Peter Schlemihl's wundersame Geschichte*.

One often hears Chamisso's poems for this cycle criticized as being old-fashioned. Perhaps for those sophisticated people who live entirely in the present they are. But is this not an indication of a lack of imagination? The rather sentimental maiden of this cycle may exaggerate her feelings, and her way of expressing them certainly is not 'modern', but is not love always a romantically exaggerated happiness or misery? Each period has its own peculiar expression. In this cycle try to forget the present and let yourself be free to enjoy the romantic sentimentality of a century which was far less matter-of-fact than our own.

You should begin the cycle with the kind of reverence and enchantment with which you might take from an old cabinet a rare piece of precious lace which had been the proud possession of your great-grandmother. You should touch it very carefully and would be rather moved as you replaced it beside the little musical clock—another relic of a bygone day.

I am certainly a modern woman and I cannot tolerate anything which is sentimental or mawkish, and yet I say: Yes, to be sure, this cycle *is* old-fashioned, but thank heaven that it is! One can never be an artist if one cannot place oneself convincingly in any atmosphere, however distant or foreign. So forget the present when you begin this cycle. Be a woman of the Biedermeier period, knowing that she loved and felt in the same way as the woman of today although she expressed herself differently.

I Seit ich ihn gesehen

The dreamy chords of the first bar reveal immediately the way in which you must sing. Out of the great melody of love which floats from your heart, the restrained chords rise with a shy subtlety like trembling sighs. Begin as if with a deep sigh. Your voice should be soft, breathy, forlorn. At 'seh' ich ihn allein' sing *ritardando* and give a soft accent to 'ihn', no *crescendo*. Accentuate 'heller' both times and exaggerate the 'h'. Your face which has been transfigured in ecstacy now becomes sad during the short interlude. You cannot quite understand the power of this magic spell which has possessed you. You cannot understand how even your dearest friends can seem so far away from you. Give your voice a darker colour. Play with the consonants in 'Schwestern' and accent 'nicht be*gehr*' ich mehr'. Sing *ritenuto* and be very careful not to slide or scoop at '*lieber* weinen still im *Kämmerlein*'. Each syllable must be very distinct. Any scooping or sliding would make it much too sentimental. Be very careful to avoid this. The last phrase—'glaub' ich blind zu sein'—is an almost whispered *pianissimo*. Your face should be radiant with a soft enchantment until the end of the postlude.

II *Er, der Herrlichste von allen*

Now you are beginning to grow accustomed to this strange feeling of ecstasy which comes over you. You have no desire, you are contented in the knowledge of your own love, which it is impossible to share with anyone. Again and again you look with rapture at the image of your beloved which seems to be always before you and you find your greatest joy in praising his virtues, his wonderful character and his great beauty. This absolute lack of passionate desire makes it possible for you to be completely happy in your love.

Begin this second song joyfully, radiantly, almost dizzy with delight. The first phrase is like a victory fanfare. Sing with absolute accuracy in exact rhythm. Each time you emphasize another of your beloved's wonderful qualities make an ecstatic accent: '*Holde* Lippen, *klares* Auge'. You feel he is so far away, so far above you—like a star in the sky. You know that it would be futile to desire a star, futile to desire this starlike image of the one and only being whom you love. But you are sad that you are not more beautiful, more worthy of him. Sing the next phrase 'So wie dort in blauer Tiefe' in the shadow of this thought and give an accent to 'fern' (consonants!) with a certain hesitancy as if it gives you pain to say 'he is so far away'. But in the interlude you return to your inner contentment.

Sing 'Wandle, wandle deine Bahnen' with nobility and with a warm flow. Bring out the lovely crescendo and *subito piano*: 'deinen Schein, nur in Demut' and accent 'Demut'.

In the next phrase the *ritardando* at 'selig nur und traurig sein' becomes *a tempo* but sing *piano*, softly, with restraint. You are overwhelmed, intoxicated by your own humility. You long to sacrifice yourself, you long to feel small and insignificant and worthless at his feet. 'Hoher Stern der Herrlichkeit' should be sung with ecstatic exuberance. Your love is boundless—you even enjoy talking about the happy woman whom he will take for his wife! But sing these phrases with inner restraint in spite of your willingness to sacrifice yourself, in spite of not really daring to imagine any happiness for yourself. 'Darf beglücken deine Wahl' has a very discreet *crescendo*. Give the most restrained *pianissimo* possible to 'und ich will die Hohe segnen'. 'Tausend mal' should have a warm *mezzoforte*. Accentuate '*wei*nen' (consonants!). 'Selig, selig bin ich dann' has a *crescendo*—it is as if you are saying to yourself. 'Oh yes, I shall be happy in *his* happiness . . .' Give a *subito piano* to 'sollte mir das Herz auch brechen', almost in tears, and now you lay your sacrifice at his feet: 'brich, o Herz, was liegt daran?' Sing this broadly, *forte*, with an almost religious quality.

The interlude brings you back to the ecstatic enthusiasm with which you began. But do not sing it with quite the same innocent joy: in the meantime you have lived in your imagination through *his* happiness and your renunciation. You have wanted to sacrifice your own heart, your own life, for him. There must now be a very subtle difference in the way in which you sing these phrases. Sing them fervently, with a delight which is almost on the verge of tears.

In the postlude your whole being should be transfigured by an overwhelming enchantment: feel the music streaming through your body, follow the musical line with your expression—but never overstep the limits which the style of Lieder singing imposes.

III *Ich kann's nicht fassen, nicht glauben*

This short breathless song should be sung as if you had just stopped running. You are so completely overwhelmed and stunned by your happiness that you have come running out of the house like a child. You are quite breathless, you cannot be sure whether this was just a dream or an intoxicating reality! Begin the song as if *plunging* into it. Sing it passionately, almost wildly. The shock has been too overwhelming—you had never, never dreamed, even in your secret heart, that he could love you.

At 'erhöht und beglückt' go over with a *ritardando* to a restrained tempo. Sing with a veiled *piano*: 'Mir war's, er habe gesprochen'. Sing this with an almost doubtful expression. You try to recall this incredible moment: yes, I *think* he said . . . And now you put your whole heart into the words 'ich bin auf ewig dein'. But immediately your doubt returns: 'Mir war's, ich träume . . .'. Sing this hurriedly, accentuated— and sing the last 'es kann ja nimmer so sein' broadly, almost in tears.

But no: it *has* been reality, it has *not* been only a dream. With this realization you throw your whole being into his life. Sing with the utmost warmth and fullness of tone, broadly, *forte*, sing it as if you were standing in the warm summer sunshine, with the warm wind blowing through your hair, flowers all about you, your arms ecstatically outstretched: 'O lass' im Traume mich sterben.'

'In Tränen unendlicher Lust' is *adagio* with a religious quality about it. The word 'Lust' must give the transition to the next phrase; sing it *ff*, ending it abruptly.

The repetition of the first phrases are now *piano*, whispered, breathy.

Don't neglect the *crescendo* at 'hat ein Traum mich berückt' but it should be more a crescendo of expression than of force. The music of the interlude must mirror your thoughts—there can be no interruption in your expression, the *music* is *you*, *you* must express the *music*. Sing the last sentence with the softest *pianissimo*, as if with tears of joy.

Hold the last note, letting it fade away gradually.

IV Du Ring an meinem Finger

This is a song of gaily animated happiness. Calm and contented in the realization of his love, you are almost childlike and as yet unawakened to passion. He loves you, how could you ask for anything more? Do you want complete surrender? Oh—you have surrendered your whole soul, your whole heart! Your heart is quiet. He, the hero of your dreams is yours forever. He shall determine your fate. You want only to follow his wishes. That is the greatest happiness for which you could ask. He has given you the ring as his betrothed. This sign of union between you is your most precious possession. You caress it, you rejoice in its unaccustomed pressure upon your finger which seems like a caress.

Begin the song in this feeling of contentment. Your voice is softly floating, light and animated. You remember the time between childhood and adolescence—'ich fand allein mich, verloren im öden, unendlichen Raum'. At this time you had no idea where you belonged. But then he came, opening the door of life and happiness for you. After 'unendlichen Raum' sing 'du' *ritenuto* and at 'Ring an meinem Finger' *a tempo*. This must be done very subtly in order to connect the phrases.

Do not misinterpret the words: 'ihm angehören ganz, hin selber mich geben'; there is neither passion nor desire here. The complete surrender of which you speak is the surrender of your soul. You have no idea of what will happen in marriage, you only know that you belong to him completely and that you will do whatever he asks of you. Sing with the deepest sincerity: 'Verklärt mich in seinem Glanz'. Sing it *ritardando* and then immediately *a tempo* at 'Ring'. (The word 'du' is still *ritardando*. Remember the same phrase earlier in the song). Accent 'Herze' and *feel* the happiness in the postlude.

V Helft mir, ihr Schwestern

The wedding day! You are surrounded by the friends of your childhood. A girl for the last time, you are in your room under your father's roof. You are blissfully happy and excited but you cannot entirely overcome a virginal fear no matter how much you chide yourself for it.

Begin the song with great excitement. You talk to your friends in order to quiet your inner fear. You admit the strangeness of your beloved who with passionate impatience has always longed for the wedding day. You have never felt this impatience. You have been quiet and contented in the realization of being his betrothed. A strange and frightening experience seems to lie before you; you ask your girlish friends to help you to overcome your foolish fears. Sing 'Helft mir, ihr Schwestern, helft mir verscheuchen eine törichte Bangigkeit', *piano*, whispering. Then putting these disturbing thoughts away you recall with delight the image of the man whose bride you will become today. You surrender yourself to him, in humility you bow your head. 'All the flowers are for him, for my hero! Who am I?' This is the overflowing expression of your own complete surrender. But now attired in your bridal dress, you look about you and bid your friends good-bye. You are no longer one of them. Today you close a door upon the life you shared with them and open one upon a world to which they do not as yet belong. Womanhood will now separate you from these girls. You have been like sisters. Now you say good-bye. This good-bye is like an interlude in the flow of the song as if, while stepping forward to meet the bridegroom, your feet yet hesitate upon the threshold and you glance back once more into the faces of your friends. Sing 'Aber euch Schwestern grüss ich mit Wehmut' with emotion and then continue with pride and dignity: 'Freudig scheidend aus eurer Schaar'. Your farewell has been *ritardando* but start *a tempo* at 'Freudig scheidend'. Realize that you cannot change too suddenly from one emotion to another. Do not sing 'Freudig scheidend' with a sudden plunge into radiance, sing it with happiness but there is still a last tear of your 'good-bye' in it, a last trembling sigh. This is difficult to explain but try to imagine this scene: 'Good-bye my dear friends. I have loved you and will always love you but now I am no longer one of you . . . Oh, I am happy to become the wife of my beloved. There is nothing I want more to be. I go to my marriage as if the doors of heaven were opening for me . . . Yet: Good-bye!' The tears of farewell mingle with the tears of happiness. You must *feel* this in order to express it.

The postlude is the wedding march. In your imagination you are walking to the altar in your bridal gown. You stand erect, your face uplifted, radiant—you look into the face of God who has blessed you with the wonder of love.

VI *Süsser Freund, du blickest*

You have changed. This must be very clear. The way in which you lean against the piano should be different, your body is relaxed, you are more experienced. You are a woman now who has also experienced the ecstacy of love in a sensual way. You are awakened. You know the power of passion. You know desire and fulfilment. Your choice is more vibrant. It has lost the untouched whiteness of your girlhood. Your *piano* tones are velvety and glowing.

Treat the first chords as if your husband, in whose arms you are lying, has just lifted your face to his. There are tears in your eyes as you meet his puzzled and questioning gaze. You say to him: 'Süsser Freund'. Never during the rapturous period of your betrothal have you called him 'süsser Freund'—this says so much, this tenderness, this caressing way of addressing him. In it is the maturity of your union. He is more than a lover now, he is your understanding friend, your companion for life. And he is 'süss' because you share with him all the secret enchantment, all the sensual delights of being one. Sing 'Süsser Freund' with a vibrant tone, give these two words all the glowing significance of which they are born.

Sing softly and with a lovely floating *piano*. The *crescendi* ('Lass' der feuchten Perlen' and 'freudig hell erzittern') should be sung very discreetly. 'Wie so bang' mein Bussen' should be sung with a breathy tone and then with sudden decisiveness (very subtly)—'Komm' und birg dein Antlitz'. Sing 'will in's Ohr dir flüstern' very gracefully and with a smile of secret joy.

The interlude is the confession of your secret and his response, overwhelmed with happiness.

Begin with a quiet dignity at 'Weisst du nun . . .'. Do not quicken the tempo, sing very quietly, warmly, softly. 'Du geliebter, geliebter Mann' must be sung with passion and intensity (consonants!). The interlude (*tempo* more vivid) again expresses his delight. He wants to rise, to tell you how complete will be the happiness which you share, to say so many, many things. But you stop him, holding him closer in your embrace. Sing 'Bleib' an meinem Herzen' with a sudden start, as if you are holding him back. You sing *accelerando,* with glowing passion until 'fester' (consonants!). The interlude is a moment of dreamy happiness.

With restrained tears of joy you speak of your child. Give 'der Morgen' and 'daraus dein Bildnis' a warm *crescendo.* The interlude is his glowing kiss and whispering beneath his caressing lips, you sigh—'Dein Bildnis'. Hold this, letting it fade away.

VII *An meinem Herzen*

Now you are a mother. Fate has brought you the fulfilment of human life and your happiness knows no bounds. This joyous song should be sung as if words are unimportant. Never mind what you say, never mind who listens to you. You look at the tiny infant in your arms and laugh and weep and talk and smile, all in one breath. Sing with warm sincerity 'Nur die da säugt' and guide the *ritardando* over into the joyful outburst of motherly pride: 'Nur eine Mutter'. The phrase 'o wie bedaur' ich doch den Mann' has a smiling humour. But your thoughts return immediately to your child and you talk rapidly to him with trembling joy.

The postlude is like a surging wave of happiness. Feel its sweep, take it up with your body, with your exultant face.

VIII *Nun hast du mir den ersten Schmerz getan*

But life which has showered you with so many blessings now has dealt you a blow by which your happiness has turned to ashes: your husband has died. Perhaps long years of contentment lie between this song and the last one. I always feel it this way. I always imagine that the children which you have born, are now grown up and living their own lives, as is the fate of parents. You have been happy in the thought of growing old with the companionship of your husband. But God, who has given you so much, has denied you this last blessing which life can bestow.

You are changed. Softness and sweetness have left you. The blow has been so sudden, shattering so unexpectedly your inner contentment, that you realize your grief with fury, and challenge fate as if it were an enemy. Imagine that you are kneeling beside the deathbed of the one you loved, feeling: but why? Why had he to go, leaving me to this desperate loneliness? How could he do this to me? Injustice and senseless reproach are often the utterances of a broken heart.

Your voice is harsh, lacking in any loveliness. There is a dark rebellion in it. You stand erect, motionless. Your eyes are wide with horror. At 'Es blicket die Verlass'ne vor sich hin' consciousness returns to you, your eyes lose their frightening expression. Sing 'Die Welt ist leer, ist leer' with what the French call 'voix blanche'. Hold the first 'leer' long enough to sound a discord with the accompaniment.

Now you go over into an austere *piano* until 'nicht lebend mehr'. In this phrase a dark resignation comes over you. You sing *piano* with a softer and darker quality. Hold 'Schleier' in the same way as you did 'leer' but softly and give an accent to 'fällt'. Visualize the *finality* in this word 'fällt': life in its fullness has ended for you, there is no longer any present or future, there is only the past. Sing very slowly, very distinctly and with a dark, velvety, veiled *pianissimo*: 'Da hab' ich dich und mein verlor'nes Glück—du meine Welt'. Give great emphasis (but very subtly) to these last words, especially 'du meine Welt'. You stand very quietly until the end of the long post-lude. You are like a statue of mourning. An incident which I recall may help to make clear to you the impression which your attitude should give here. Long ago a wonderful friend of mine died. He was buried near Vienna in a remote little graveyard surrounded by forests and mountains. He had loved this spot and wanted to be buried there, far from the world. But he had been a great artist and hundreds of people came from Vienna to attend his funeral. His grave was high up on the slope of a hill. As we followed his flower-laden coffin I watched his widow climbing behind the pall-bearers. She was a fragile little woman but the terrible grief of losing her husband could not crush her. She walked upwards with an heroic erectness, a noble dignity, her face uplifted to the hill where the open grave lay. She seemed to have the grandeur of a Greek statue. This is the impression which you must convey throughout the postlude, while the music tells of the past.

LIEDERKREIS

ROBERT SCHUMANN

The Eichendorff *Liederkreis*—not to be confused with the *Liederkreis* to poems by Heine—was composed in 1840.

JOSEPH FREIHERR VON EICHENDORFF

Born at Lubowitz in Silesia in 1788, died at Neisse in Silesia, 1857. He was a central figure of the German Romantic movement, the author of numerous poems with a strong feeling for the countryside and a folk-song quality.

One cannot really call this Liederkreis a 'cycle'. The songs are not related to one another, and yet they share, so to speak, a unity, since they are the work of a single poet, Eichendorff.

I IN DER FREMDE

You look into the distance where beyond the red lightning which threatens your world, your old home lies, far beyond the horizon. The clouds drift towards you as if sent by friends, but you know better: nobody remembers you there. None of your old circle is still living. Your parents have been dead long since. As you sing you realize that you are speaking of a distant past. Do not put too much emotion and sadness into the words 'Aber Vater und Mutter sind lange tot'. It is such an eternity ago that they died! Time has healed your sadness, for time is the great healer. And you say to yourself that soon the time will come for you, too, to be laid to rest. The forest which you have loved so dearly will sing its lovely melody above your grave, and you will rest in peace to this eternal lullaby. You feel no fear; you feel only the consolation that your rest will be beautiful and undisturbed. You enjoy the thought of your life's ending because you will be less lonely in your everlasting sleep than you are now in your worldly loneliness.

II INTERMEZZO

This song is born of a deep and serene happiness. Sing it as if it were a love letter, starting with a warm *pianissimo*. When you sing: 'Mein Herz tief in sich singet ein altes schönes Lied', you remind your beloved that you have sung it together. And now it found its way to you, rising into the air and flying on wings of love to her. The *accelerando* at 'Das in die Luft sich schwinget', should have an exuberant feeling. The ending should be broad and full of loving devotion.

III WALDESGESPRÄCH

On quiet summer days when the Rhine lies like a broad shimmering band of silk in the sunlight, the beautiful witch Lorelei mounts her milk-white horse and rides through the dark forest. She hates the peaceful, silvery water; she hates the boats which pass so quietly; she hates the smiling faces of the fishermen who could now in safety marvel at her beauty, when she sits upon her rock, hoping to destroy them. So she turns towards the silent forest, riding slowly through the deep ferns, lost in brooding thought. A young man, carefree and gay, passes through the woods. He has lost his way, but he knows that he will find it again for already he can hear the bugle calls of his friends who are searching for him. Suddenly his horse stops, trembling with fright. There before him, on a white horse, is a woman, lovely as a dream. Golden hair floats about her beautiful face; her eyes burn darkly and strangely. The young man does not feel the strangeness of this unreal apparition. With strong, calm hands he reins in his trembling horse and laughingly looks into the deep, dark flames of her eyes. Adventure seems to beckon to him. How beautiful she is! How strangely and challengingly she looks at him! The blood pulses through his veins. Boldly, sure of victory, he addresses this lovely woman.

Begin the song with great fire and assurance. The accompaniment is the melody of his life. Apparently he is a man of strong will, accustomed to get what he wants. At the moment it is this strangely seductive woman whom he desires. She seems to be a willing prey. But she answers him with words which seem to glide over him like the murmur of the swaying trees. Her first phrases should be sung without expression, with half-closed eyes, gazing, so to speak, above the head of the impetuous youth into the emptiness of space. Imagine that you, the singer, are like the evil spirit of the sombre forest, the whispering voice of a dangerous wilderness, a wilderness in which fern and clinging vines grow, where snakes under the thick moist leaves rear their heads awaiting their prey.

The warning: 'O flieh! Du weisst nicht, wer ich bin', should be sung with the intention not of warning, but of luring him.

The young man is adventurous. He does not fear danger; on the contrary, he is intrigued by it. Perhaps others have been lost in this wilderness, their piercing cries for help ringing out through the forest. But he is sure of himself; he knows how to deal with danger; he welcomes it. And you, the clever Lorelei, know, that if you warn him of danger, he will never give up. His answer comes back with the same straightforward, gay melody of the beginning. He does not even listen to her words. He is intoxicated by the beauty of Lorelei. Determined to take her in his arms, he approaches her. Then suddenly, in a flash, he recognizes her. He sees the witch of whom he has heard ever since his childhood, the witch of the fairy-tales that were told to him as he sat on his mother's lap beside the fireplace, the witch of whom the fishermen tell as they sit mending their nets on the banks of the Rhine, the witch of whom young girls tell as they sit together at their spinning wheels on winter evenings. The young lad had really never believed these stories. 'Fairy-tales!' he used to scoff laughingly. But now he looks into the terrifying eyes of the witch herself. He crosses himself, knowing that God alone can help him to escape her hypnotic gaze.

Here you must slowly raise yourself, becoming from head to toe the triumphant witch Lorelei herself. 'Yes, I am Lorelei; you know me well. You know my castle high above the Rhine!' Sing this in a tone of icy triumph—and then with fierce scorn, repeating the impetuous words which the young man had used when he first caught sight of her, when he was so sure of himself and so confident of an easy conquest of her. Sing this with cutting irony: 'Es ist schon spät, es ist schon kalt', and end triumphantly: 'Kommst nimmermehr aus diesem Wald'. The repetitions of 'nimmermehr' should be like hammer blows. Keep your expression of dark and triumphant hatred until the end of the postlude. This fades away into the first theme of the young lad, but it is only a recollection of his carefree laughter. You feel—and your listeners must feel it with you— that his laughter dies on his pale lips even as the melody fades away and that the deep ferns will close around his lifeless body like a web, that nevermore will the forest release the prey of Lorelei.

IV DIE STILLE

This whole song should have no real *forte* tone. You tell yourself the secret of your heart. You are so very happy, only you know why. And only one other person should know it: your beloved. Your thoughts are dancing, are flying like birds far over the seas of the world till you are in heaven, and heaven is the nearness of him whom you love. Nobody knows about this glowing, secret love, nobody will ever know it. You do not care if *he* were the only one to know.

V MONDNACHT

This song is generally sung like a difficult 'vocalize' in which the soaring *pianissimo* seems to be all-important. But you should never approach a Lied or an aria only from the vocally technical point of view. Pure technique may be the mark of an excellent *singer*. It is not enough to make an *artist*.

You must feel the poetical mood of the moonlit night. Heaven and earth seem to be united in a serene embrace. The whole mysterious beauty of the night is carried on the wings of music over the slumbering earth, and your soul has wings and spreads them out and flies over the earth as if it were flying homewards. Between the words 'Und meine Seele spannte weit ihre Flügel aus', there is a musical break which you have to bridge. Link with your breath the word 'spannte' to the next words, 'weit ihre Flügel aus'. A generous *crescendo* will carry the phrase over to the next phrase to which it so obviously belongs, making it especially beautiful and important. This, the expression of your own soul, is the only *crescendo* in the whole song, but if you build up to this climax, it will be overwhelmingly lovely.

VI SCHÖNE FREMDE

Mysterious and strange is the night in this song. Here are the ruins of an old castle where Gods have reigned long, long ago. The phrase 'Hier unter den Myrthenbäumen in heimlich dämmernder Pracht' must be sung with a great sweeping *crescendo* growing out of *pianissimo*. It is as if wings were soaring over the ruins of the old castle. When you sing 'Was sprichst du wirr, wie in Träumen, zu mir, phantastische Nacht', *you* really are the dreamer who listens with bated breath to the strangely quiet night. All the stars seem to look down on you and from far away it is as if you can hear a voice telling you that great happiness will soon come to you. This wonderful, soaring promise should be sung with a sweeping *forte*.

VII AUF EINER BURG

This whole song must be sung in a very subdued and mysterious *pianissimo*. *There is no crescendo whatsoever*. Only if you do it thus will the song make sense and, of course, effect. The old Emperor Barbarossa has been turned to stone, and has sat for centuries upon his stone throne. Only the birds are alive. They sit in the empty windows.

A wedding party passes, far down below the mountains, along the Rhine. But in spite of the gay music of the band, the lovely bride is weeping. She alone feels the emptiness of the world around her. She alone becomes part of this empty loneliness.

VIII IN DER FREMDE

Sing this song with a secret and whispering intimacy. You have lost your way—not only here in this lonely forest, but in the world. Everything comes to you as in a dream. The castle where you were so happy long ago seems to lie at your feet, but you know that this cannot be; it is so far away. And you see your beloved in the flower garden, knowing that she has been long dead and will never wait for you as she had promised; only in a dream will she be with you, or in the torment of your mind.

IX WEHMUT

I am very much against sentimentality and again and again I remind my students that through sentimentality they only weaken and destroy the greatness of a song. Approaching this song a student said to me with shining eyes: 'But now at last I can be sentimental!' and I had to answer 'Yes'. But I would prefer to call this sentimentality emotion. Do not overdo it by sliding down from one syllable to the next. The song should never lose its quiet, melancholy nobility.

X ZWIELICHT

Your heart is full of doubt and foreboding. Everything in nature which should be beautiful and calming to a sane mind seems here distorted. Whisper the phrase: 'Was will dieses Grauen bedeuten?' You do not sense the serene calm of the forest; you only hear, in your imagination, hunters who want to kill what you love. You do not even trust your best friend any longer; he may be kind to you, but you see, behind his kindness, only deceit. There is one moment of relief. Tomorrow there will be reborn what today is lost and gone. But immediately your doubts return. The night will swallow all that you had hoped for. Therefore: beware, be watchful, and do not sleep.

XI IM WALDE

You see a wedding party coming over the mountain. The band is playing, the birds join in the gay melodies, it sounds so happy and gay. But before you can realize it, the music dies away, the picture of the wedding procession vanishes— and night falls. Only the forest whispers its old melody, and you feel very lonely and your heart trembles within you.

XII FRÜHLINGSNACHT

But the 'cycle', if one can so describe it, ends on a happy note. This is a song with which very often a concert programme is closed. It is such a sweeping and gay song, it is so full of life and springtime happiness, that it seems quite irresistible to any singer or audience.

Spring has come, the wandering birds are back, and the first flowers are already blooming in the valley. You would like to shout for joy, and at the same time weep for joy, because you can scarcely believe it. Your beloved is yours! All nature sings with you, moon and stars, the forest, the nightingales—all sing to you: 'Sie ist deine, sie ist dein!'

MAGELONELIEDER
Romanzen aus *Magelone*

JOHANNES BRAHMS

Born in Hamburg, 1833; died in Vienna, 1897. Brahms epitomizes the late Romantic spirit and this cycle is arch-Romantic both in subject and treatment. The first six songs in the cycle were published in 1865, and the remaining nine in 1869.

LUDWIG TIECK

Born in Berlin, 1773 and died there in 1853. He might be described as the moving spirit of early Romantic poetry in Germany, but he is equally celebrated for his numerous short stories, novels and plays. His famous translation of Shakespeare's plays (with A. W. Schlegel) did much to popularize the great dramatist's work in Germany.

I Keinen hat es noch gereut

Count Peter of Provence is a strikingly handsome youth. He lives with his parents in an old castle and could be happy there forever. But a wandering Minstrel has instilled in him a longing to see the wide world with its adventures and dangers. The Minstrel sang: 'Keinen hat es noch gereut'. The song starts with a fanfare and you sing very gaily: 'Keinen hat es noch gereut, der das Ross bestiegen'. Sing it with your *full* voice. The accompaniment illustrates the galloping horse and this rhythm runs through the whole song. The interlude starts *forte* and dies away into *piano*, as if horse and rider are disappearing in the distance. Then start *piano*: 'Berge und Auen, einsamer Wald', and with a slowly developing *crescendo* the world seems to open up before the rider. *Pianissimo* again: 'Wunderlich fliehen Gestalten dahin', and the longing which has awakened in him is quiet and subdued. But his horse gallops on, and he experiences fame and the love of beautiful women. Here again a slow *crescendo* brings him to a climax of delight. Enemies envy his easy victories, but humbly he chooses the one girl he truly loves. On gallops his horse as he leaves behind him the scenes—and victims—of his conquests in love and war. Many years later he will tell his son of all he has seen and lived through and he will show him with pride his scars of battle. Even in old age the memory of his romantic youth casts a glow over the twilight of his life.

The postlude brings back the rhythm of the galloping horse and fades away, as the voice vanishes into dreams and sleep.

II Traun! Bogen und Pfeil

Peter sings happily as he rides along. Life is good, his enemies lie defeated, so his song sounds carefree and happy. 'Traun! Bogen und Pfeil sind gut für den Feind'. This is an uncomplicated song. Sing *forte* the lusty verse which is repeated several times.

III Sind es Schmerzen, sind es Freuden

Peter arrives in Naples where tournaments are being held and he asks to take part in them. There he sees the beautiful Magelone for the first time and falls in love with her. She is the daughter of the king and is watching the tournament from her place of honour. Peter is victorious and overthrows many knights. The king is delighted with him and Magelone looks smilingly into his eyes. Peter is deeply in love and sings of it with a trembling heart: 'Sind es Schmerzen, sind es Freuden'. The song starts *pianissimo* very softly and somewhat hesitantly, but very soon develops into a swinging *fortissimo*. The whole song should be sung with complete abandon. It is as if a spring storm floods through Peter's heart. Start *piano* when you sing: 'Tausend neue Blumen blüh'n'. The second verse starts and develops like the first. *Piano, crescendo,* full *forte.* But soon Peter realizes that Magelone may not be for him. What can he expect? There are tears in his eyes: 'Ach und fällt die Träne nieder', he sings in a hushed voice. There are pauses between each word. Do not exaggerate them. Your breath seems to falter, but if you do it too obviously then you will distort the passionate feeling of unworthiness which Peter experiences. Life seems to him now like a grave. But then, suddenly, he starts up in defiance: 'Ohne Verschulden soll ich erdulden?' He does not understand himself any more. Even in his dreams he is torn between different emotions and his desperate cry: 'Ich kenne mich noch kaum', is as if in self-accusation. There is one thing which he knows as deepest truth: his love for Magelone. Come what may, he must love her—and her alone.

And so he swears to stars and world and love a holy oath: 'Ach nur im Licht von ihrem Blick wohnt Leben und Hoffnung und Glück'. And his oath echoes through the world: 'Bleib' ich ihr ferne, sterb' ich gerne!'

IV Liebe kam aus fernen Landen

Peter was happy to see Magelone's nurse in church. He begged her to give to her mistress a poem he had written; and to show his appreciation to the messenger, he presented her with one of the precious rings his mother had given him as her farewell present. Magelone urged her faithful nurse to give her the ring which she then put on a thin string of pearls and wore it round her neck. She read and re-read Peter's poem with joy and longing.

Start this song at a steady 'walking' rhythm, and when you sing 'schlang mich ein mit süssen Banden', do it with a *swinging* rhythm. Be careful to watch the stressed first notes at the repetition of this phrase.

Magelone is touched by his loneliness at the words: 'Wozu dieses Spielen?' Then comes a much more vivid tempo, with a singing *rubato*, at: 'Alle meine Wünsche flogen'. The next phrase: 'Ach, wer löst nun meine Ketten?' must be sung with passion and *morendo* at: 'Keiner will mich retten!' But Peter pleads with her and sings 'Wenn die Eine dich nicht liebt, bleibt nur bitt'rer Tod dem Kranken'.

The accompanying music dies away to nothing at the end.

V *So willst du des Armen*

The nurse is clever enough to meet Peter again in church, and he gives her a second ring for her mistress, and another poem, which Magelone reads with great emotion.

The short prelude is like a cry of joy. Sing with abandon and in a steady *crescendo*: 'So willst du des Armen dich gnädig erbarmen? So ist es kein Traum?'

Then, almost whispering: 'Wie rieseln die Quellen'. The next phrases again have short pauses between the words and—as before—this is meant to express the *breathtaking* happiness and has to be sung with this idea. Don't exaggerate!

'Mein schüchtern' Gesicht' is very *legato* and *piano*.

The song develops slowly from *piano* to a jubilant *forte* at the end.

VI *Wie soll ich die Freude*

Peter waited the next morning at the church, and his hopes were justified; the nurse came again, and told him that her mistress was longing for him. Peter was beside himself with happiness. Then she said that if he would swear a holy oath that his intentions were pure and virtuous, she would arrange a meeting of the lovers in her own chamber. With this promise, she left the knight, and jubilantly he sang: 'Wie soll ich die Freude, die Wonne denn tragen!'

The prelude—a strong *allegro*—expresses Peter's happiness: 'Wie soll ich die Freude, die Wonne denn tragen? Dass unter dem Schlagen des Herzens die Seele nicht scheide?' And the short interlude repeats the same melody as the prelude. Yet Peter cannot trust his good fortune and asks himself how life could be endured if everything were to prove an empty illusion. Time passes so slowly—tomorrow seems so far away. The accompaniment imitates the heavy tread of time, but at the words: 'Und wenn ich werde scheiden müssen, wie federleicht fliegt dann ihr Tritt', it runs light-footed. The 'featherlight' tempo passes to *poco sostenuto*, after a slow *ritardando*.

VII Schlage, sehnsüchtige Gewalt

Sing now with emotion and great warmth: 'Schlage, sehnsüchtige Gewalt, in tiefer, treuer Brust'. Peter complains that soon all happiness will be forgotten and the stream of time will change from today to tomorrow. But he takes fresh courage and (with a broad *crescendo*) he sings: 'Will es nun auch weiter wagen, wie es werden will'.

The short interlude leads to a more animated tempo with his conviction that he really has no cause for doubt. Love will be his companion to the end of his life.

The piano music starts now like a whispered promise and Peter sings of the happiness which awaits him. And the long song ends with a soaring *crescendo*.

VIII War es dir, dem diese Lippen bebten

At last the long-awaited moment came, and Peter gave Magelone the third and most precious ring as a sign of their betrothal. Magelone kissed Peter who, startled and happy, returned the kiss. Then he hurried home and sang to his lute: 'War es dir, dem diese Lippen bebten?'

The song starts like a simple folk melody. If happiness is too great, perhaps there is comfort in expressing one's emotions in quiet words and gentle music. Peter tries to be calm, but soon his passion overwhelms him: 'Ha! Wie Licht und Glanz vor meinen Augen schwebten, alle Sinne nach den Lippen strebten'. He sees the longing in her eyes, and the whole world seems to sing love songs: '. . . und die süssen Worte gar weckten das tiefste Verlangen'. Peter feels like dying on her kiss, but it would have been the most wonderful death at this most intoxicating moment.

IX *Wir müssen uns trennen*

Magelone's father, the King of Naples, wishes her to marry the knight Heinrich von Carpone. He orders a great tournament in which Carpone should show his courage and then be rewarded with Magelone's hand. But in this tournament Peter is victorious over Carpone. Magelone has to tell her fiancé that her father still wishes her to marry Carpone. She asks him to flee with her secretly. So Peter returns home to prepare for the flight and to take farewell of his lute. He sings 'Wir müssen uns trennen'.

The song starts with some chords. Then the accompaniment imitates the lute, and Peter sings: 'Wir müssen uns trennen, geliebtes Saitenspiel'. His heart is beating in anticipation of his flight with Magelone. He speaks to his trusty weapons in a march-like rhythm. He does not wait to take a boat but throws himself impatiently into the sea, sure of himself, of his powerful arms. He does not lack courage and is proud of his valour. But now he listens to the quiet sound of his lute and dreams of the coming night and of the laughing morning sun.

X *Ruhe, Süssliebchen*

Peter waits for Magelone. He has three horses, one for each of them, and one carrying provisions. Magelone has brought some precious possessions, chief among them the three rings which she wears on a pearl necklace. They ride through the night and all the next day, but now Magelone is weary. They stop and Peter sings to her a lovely cradle-song: 'Ruhe, Süssliebchen!'

The song starts slowly and in a tender *pianissimo*: 'Ruhe,

Süssliebchen, im Schatten der grünen, dämmernden Nacht'. The accompanying music is soft and peaceful as it sways with the voice. There is not one harsh note in voice or piano, only a slight *crescendo* at 'schlafe, schlaf'ein'. And this *crescendo* should be like a wave, floating up and down. After 'ewig bin ich dein' there follows a short interlude which fades from a soft *piano* into *pianissimo*. And so again, after 'ich will dein Wächter sein'. Then comes a more animated tempo at 'Murmelt fort, ihr Melodieen', but to the end of the song everything is *pianissimo*. The postlude dies away with a soft *ritardando*.

XI *So tönet denn, schäumende Wellen*

There are birds among the branches of the tree under which Magelone is sleeping. They chirp very softly as if not to disturb the slumbering girl. She had put her necklace with the three rings carefully beside her on the grass. Suddenly a raven swoops down and flies away with the precious jewels. Peter, alarmed and angry, follows the bird and throws stones at it in the hope that it will abandon its loot; but the raven flies towards the sea. Peter finds an old abandoned boat and continues his pursuit of the raven which at last drops the necklace into the water. A sudden storm arises as Peter desperately hunts for the lost necklace in the sea. The land now is far distant, and evening draws on. Peter feels utterly lost. He sings with a loud, sad voice: 'So tönet denn, schäumende Wellen'.

The song starts (and continues) in a stormy *allegro*. Peter speaks to the cruel sea: 'Mag Unglück doch laut um mich bellen, erbost sein das grausame Meer'.

In the piano music there is the sound of surging waves. Peter is at the mercy of the sea. 'Denn nimmer wird es gut!' This helpless cry is followed by a short interlude which starts *forte* and moderates into *piano* and *ritardando*. The music sounds here like a sigh of desperation.

For Peter there comes a moment of resignation: 'Nicht klag' ich, und mag ich nun scheitern, in wäss'rigen Tiefen vergeh'n, mein Blick wird nie sich mehr erheitern, den Stern meiner Liebe zu seh'n'. But he ends with a cry of desperation: 'Ich bin ein verlorener Mann!'

He gives up hope, lies down in the boat and waits for death.

XII *Muss es eine Trennung geben*

A large vessel approaches the small boat where Peter is lying—a heathen, Moorish crew. They rescue Peter and bring him to the Sultan. He is not kept there as a slave, because the Sultan is much impressed by him and makes him superintendent of his gardens. In the evening Peter often takes a zither and sings, thinking of his beloved Magelone: 'Muss es eine Trennung geben'. The music here is continuously *poco andante*, with the sound of the accompanying zither, and the voice floating over it in a lovely *legato*.

XIII *Geliebter, wo zaudert dein irrender Fuss*

The Sultan has a beautiful daughter, Sulima. She falls in love with Peter who remains faithful to his Magelone. But his longing for home is strong and, thinking that Magelone may have died in the forest where he had to leave her, he listens to Sulima's blandishments. She tells him that she will elope with him and will give him a sign at the right moment. She will sing on her zither: 'Geliebter, wo zaudert dein irrender Fuss?'

The prelude is secret, mysterious. In it is all the alluring beauty of the Sultan's daughter. 'Geliebter, wo zaudert dein irrender Fuss? Die Nachtigall plaudert von Sehnsucht und Kuss'. Throughout the whole song, Sulima is searching for Peter, but he has taken a boat and is already far away at sea. His thoughts are only for his betrothed, Magelone. He has found new courage and a new determination to find his home, to find *her*, at last to find happiness.

A large sailing boat approaches. He is afraid that the crew are Moors and that they will take him back to the Sultan and to Sulima. But they are Christians and are sailing to France.

Peter's parents were very sad to have had no news from him. But one day a fisherman brought a fish for their dinner and, to their astonishment, when it was cut open, they found the three rings in its stomach—the three rings his mother had given Peter as a farewell gift. Now the parents were sure they would see their son again.

XIV Wie schnell verschwindet so Licht und Glanz

In the meantime Magelone awakened and found Peter gone. She thought despairingly that he had abandoned her, until she found the three horses still tied to the tree. She realized now that Peter must have been the victim of some misfortune and wandered off through the forest. She searched for Peter and eventually came to the hut of a shepherd and his wife. She had disguised herself by concealing her long golden hair under a scarf and covering her face with a veil. The shepherd and his wife took her into their humble home, and there she often sat at her spinning-wheel in front of the door and sang: 'Wie schnell verschwindet so Licht und Glanz!'

The prelude starts with a very simple melody, but a dark cloud passes over it at the words: 'Die Sonne neiget, die Röte flieht, der Schatten steiget, und Dunkel zieht'.

Magelone is deeply unhappy and ends her song thus: 'Vom schönen Lande weit weg gebracht zum öden Strande wo um uns Nacht . . .'

XV Treue Liebe dauert lange

In the meantime Peter has landed on a small island where the sailing boat has anchored. But he falls asleep in a flowery meadow, and the boat sails away without him. Awaking, he realizes what has happened, and falls to the ground in a swoon.

Some fishermen find him and bring him to a shepherd's hut where he will find kindly people who will help him. But—in the best Romantic tradition—it is not help he finds but his Magelone. United at last, the lovers return to Peter's home and there they are married.

At the spot where Peter first met Magelone he builds a great palace and the shepherd and his wife are well rewarded. They visit this palace each year and sing: 'Treue Liebe dauert lange'. Their song begins and ends like a chorale: 'Treue Liebe dauert lange, sie scheidet vom Leide, und nimmer entschwinde die liebliche, selige, himmlische Lust!'

All lived happily ever after—and if they have not died, no doubt they are still living happily!

VIER ERNSTE GESÄNGE

JOHANNES BRAHMS

The *Vier ernste Gesänge* were Brahms' last composition and were written in 1896.

The words are taken from Luther's translation of the Bible—the first three songs from the Book of Ecclesiastes and the fourth song from the first book of Corinthians.

I Denn es gehet dem Menschen wie dem Vieh
(Eccles. iii, 19–22)

The first song starts with a heavy, floating, simple melody. At first the man who rebels against God's word sings with subdued and colourless tone, but soon his anger expresses itself in a strong *crescendo* and *decrescendo*. The last words—'denn es ist alles eitel'—are followed by a tumult in the accompaniment. It is the turmoil in his soul—the desperate struggle of hope and faith against cynicism and anger. 'Es fährt alles an einen Ort, es ist alles von Staub gemacht und wird wieder zu Staub'. These phrases are interrupted by the piano which tells him that he lies to himself. And when you sing: 'Wer weiss ob der Geist des Menschen aufwärts fahre!' you feel the deep doubt in his heart. (*Perhaps* it is as we have been taught—perhaps, perhaps . . .) But the interlude once more is full of doubt—and the heavy, strong chords: 'Und der Odem des Viehes unterwärts unter die Erde fahre?' are again a sign of inner questioning. Here in the accompaniment he realizes that work is the best gift a man can have, that he should be happy in achieving his purpose. There he stands already on the threshold of understanding and of surrender. But the insistent question returns stormily at the words: 'Denn wer will ihn dahin bringen, dass er sehe, was nach ihm geschehen wird?' A man who is deeply convinced that men and animals must, in the end, share the same fate would never mention the fact that there are people who can believe what *he* cannot and will not believe.

The accompaniment rages throughout this searching question, until, like the calm after a storm, it dies down in the last two bars. The song closes with two harsh chords.

II Ich wandte mich und sah an alle
(Eccles. iv, 1–3)

The man who has always thought only of himself, and of his own unhappy lot, looks around and feels compassion for those who suffer injustice. He has already taken one step forward towards wisdom, the knowledge that we all are in the hands of the Lord, the Creator of us all. The accompanying music is soft and floats with your voice in tender *crescendi* and *decrescendi*. The man cannot see that those who suffer could ever find a word or a deed that may console him, for those who made him suffer are too powerful. Very *pianissimo*, he says: 'Da lobte ich die Toten die schon gestorben waren'. The accompaniment hesitates to follow these hopeless words and you sing with deep emotion. Even those who never were born are to be praised, because they do not know how much injustice is done under the sun. This injustice affects him so profoundly that he ends the song almost in tears—tears of a compassion which will guide him towards a better understanding.

III O Tod, wie bitter bist du
(Eccles. xli, 1–2)

In the next song his sense of injustice tells him that the man who has everything in life will suffer the bitterness of death. It seems to me that this resembles the story of the poor man who looked at the palaces of the rich and said to himself: 'But I am sure they are unhappy. For their death will be terrible'. So this man imagines that death is much more bitter for the rich and the happy than for himself and for all those who are his brothers in poverty.

The accompaniment has only two *crescendi* here after the heavy *fortissimo* at the beginning. First a *crescendo* at 'wenn an dich gedenket ein Mensch', and a second and stronger one at 'und dem es wohl geht in allen Dingen und noch wohl essen mag!' There is also a *ritenuto* when you sing out loudly again: 'O Tod, wie bitter bist du!' The key changes and with it the tone of your voice, to a much lighter and more silvery quality:

'O Tod, wie wohl tust du dem Dürftigen'. The accompaniment floats in a lovely *legato* and turns to a dark and brooding sound at 'dem Dürftigen, der da schwach und alt ist'. The doubt returns here with a harsh *crescendo*: 'und nichts Besseres zu hoffen noch zu erwarten hat'. The last words: 'O Tod, wie wohl tust du', are like a blessing, a pious chorale; and yet he is still far from real understanding.

IV Wenn ich mit Menschen- und mit Engelszungen redete
(I Cor. xiii, 1–3, 12–13)

With the opening chords, like a fanfare, this song announces St Paul's great declaration of truth and happiness. You sing with great and joyous conviction what he has learned through a lifetime of struggle, of delusions, and of doubts. But now he understands, now he has found satisfaction and humility. 'Wenn ich mit Menschen- und mit Engelszungen redete, und hätte der Liebe nicht, so wär' ich ein tönend' Erz oder eine klingende Schelle'. 'Liebe' is the climax of the phrase and must stand out as such. It is the love for God, for the world, for his neighbour, for everything and everyone around him.... And now he enjoys telling again and again of deeds and words which would be nothing without *love*.

The piano accompanies the voice as gradually each phase of understanding is reached. After the last 'So wäre mir's nichts nütze', the music dies away in a soft *ritardando*. Then the key changes and you sing very *legato* and with deep emotion: 'Wir sehen jetzt durch einen Spiegel in einem dunkeln Worte'. We see the world which we searched for only in a dark mirror—but then we shall see it face to face with the Lord. Now we only see it partly, but then we shall know as much as we have been known. The key changes again and you sing very distinctly: 'Nun aber bleibet Glaube, Hoffnung, Liebe, diese drei'. Each word is *sforzato*—and then sing with the softest expression: 'Aber die Liebe ist die grösseste unter ihnen'.

The song ends with a great *ritardando*.

WESENDONCKLIEDER

RICHARD WAGNER

Born in Leipzig, 1813; died in Venice, 1883. This cycle is virtually Wagner's only contribution to the literature of Lieder except for some early songs dating from before the composition of *Rienzi*. These five songs are themselves, so to speak, sketches for his operas; the first and fourth for *Die Walküre* and the remaining three for *Tristan*. The cycle exists in both piano and orchestral versions.

MATHILDE WESENDONCK

Born at Elberfeld in 1828, died at Traunblick, 1902. She met Wagner in Zürich, and their relationship exercised a profound influence on him, culminating in the composition of *Tristan und Isolde*. She is remembered today only by these five poems which Wagner set during the period 1857 to 1862.

I DER ENGEL

The song starts with a softly soaring melody which accompanies the words 'In der Kindheit frühen Tagen hört' ich oft von Engeln sagen, die des Himmels hehre Wonne tauschen mit der Erdensonne, dass, wo bang ein Herz in Sorgen schmachtet vor der Welt verborgen, dass, wo still es will verbluten, und vergeh'n in Tränenfluten, dass, wo brünstig sein Gebet einzig um Erlösung fleht'. Raise your voice in *emotion*, not in *volume*; and when you sing 'da der Engel niederschwebt, und es sanft gen Himmel hebt', the accompaniment soars upwards with your voice. Until now you have told of the *legend*. But now you come to *yourself* and with this, your emotion rises in expression, but always in tender *pianissimo*: 'Ja, es stieg auch mir ein Engel nieder, und auf leuchtendem Gefieder führt er, ferne jedem Schmerz, meinen Geist nun himmelwärts'. Who could that angel be but Wagner? The shimmering wings are bearers of the music which he created and which carries the poet away from the earth with its conventions and restrictions—upwards, to what, for her, is *heaven*.

The postlude, with its *crescendo* and *decrescendo*, seems like a hymn of freedom and release.

II STEHE STILL!

The next song is an impassioned address to all creation. It is too much to endure, too much to see the fierce will of creative power. Each plea is like a cry for mercy. The *crescendi* and *decrescendi* are like beating waves, and when you sing: 'Genug des Werdens, lass' mich sein!', you express yourself in full *fortissimo*. But it is not yet enough. Your plea continues, creation will not let you rest. At last you sing again of love and peaceful serenity, and the music, accompanying your words, is soft and gentle. The wonder of love has made you understand the wonder of the world. And with gradually increasing power you end the song with the inner conviction that you have solved the riddle and have recognized the will of God over the laws of nature.

III IM TREIBHAUS

Perhaps I may be permitted here a brief digression. I was engaged to sing the five Wagner songs in Vienna under the baton of Maestro Toscanini. I was terrified of singing 'Im Treibhaus' with him, knowing his passion for perfection—and I felt a good deal less than perfect. But he insisted, and told me so in the following letter which I give here in French and in translation.

'. . . Pourquoi ne veux-tu pas me donner la joie de t'entendre dans "Treibhaus"? C'est de la meilleure musique de Wagner. . . . Non, tu verras que le mouvement que je vais prendre ne sera pas trop lent, et tu chanteras comme d'habitude—merveilleusement. Mais *tu dois* chanter "Im Treibhaus" et tu vas me donner de la joie. Ainsi, c'est entendu, n'est-ce pas? Sois bonne avec ton Maestro et ne sois pas nerveuse de chanter avec lui.'

('Why don't you want to give me the joy of hearing you in "Treibhaus?" This is the most beautiful music of Wagner. . . . No, you will see that the tempo I shall take will not be too slow, and you will sing as is your habit: marvellously. But you have to sing "Im Treibhaus" and you will give me this joy. So that is settled now, isn't it? Be good to your Maestro and don't be nervous of singing with him.')

Of course I sang!

The song is pervaded by a mysterious half-light. The prelude seems to breathe the faint perfume of exotic flowers. The plants seem like tall canopies of emerald. They come from distant countries; they are sad and lonely. They stretch their branches upwards like pitiful hands, and sigh. The music, too, floats upwards in softest *pianissimo*, as if guided by the trembling branches. The fragrance is sweet and scarcely perceptible. I see the poor plants stretch out their arms into nothingness. I stand there, forlorn in their midst, but I feel I am a part of them. I, too, live in splendour of light and yet I know that my home is not here. When evening comes I welcome the darkness, because those who are truly unhappy like to hide in the darkness of silence.

The music trembles in mysterious unity with the plants. A sigh floats through the wide and silent hall, and I see heavy drops like tears on the edges of the leaves. The postlude fades away and the last chords fall like drops into nothingness. . . .

IV SCHMERZEN

This whole song has something almost 'military' in its pompous outbursts. I have never liked it—especially when I heard Toscanini describe it as musically rather weak. Yet it is effective and so much a part of the unity of these five Lieder that one must include it in the cycle. With orchestra it sounds better than with piano accompaniment. (As a matter of fact, all five songs are written in an alternative version with orchestra and should be so sung.)

The song starts with a kind of triumphant fanfare and must be played with strong rhythm. Then the voice takes up the same 'military' sound with the words: 'Sonne, weinest jeden Abend dir die schönen Augen rot'—which, to my mind, is a most curious description of the glorious setting of the sun! You continue: 'Wenn im Meeresspiegel badend dich erreicht der frühe Tod'. But now with a big *crescendo* in voice and accompaniment: 'Doch erstehst in alter Pracht, Glorie der düstren Welt, du am Morgen neu erwacht, wie ein stolzer Siegesheld'.

Once more you voice your own thoughts: 'Ach, wie sollte ich da klagen, wie, mein Herz, so schwer dich seh'n, muss die Sonne selbst verzagen, muss die Sonne untergeh'n?' I always think here of Schubert's beautiful song 'Im Abendrot'. How simply he expresses the same emotion! There is no pomposity in his music, only the deep gratitude of a wise heart. But here Wagner seems to have lost his genius for subtle expression. And even the *piano* in the following phrases cannot help, for the ending is again the voice of victory: 'Und gebieret Tod nur Leben, geben Schmerzen Wonne nur, o wie dank' ich, dass gegeben solche Schmerzen mir Natur!' The song ends with a tumultuous outburst of joy until the last two bars which fade away as dreams vanish in the morning.

V TRÄUME

This song is a study for the love duet in the second act of *Tristan und Isolde*. But this 'study' is so beautiful that it has become one of the most admired Lieder of our time.

The long prelude should be played with the softest emotional expression and when the voice starts it must have the same dream-like quality. The *crescendi* are gentle and must never rise above *pianissimo*. The first 'Träume' is still very soft, and not until the following phrases is there a *crescendo* and a little *accelerando*. When you sing: 'Allvergessen, Eingedenken!' give great importance to these two words. They are really the *high-point* of the song. (To forget the world with its trivialities, to realize instead what is serious and all-important for you, that is the meaning of these two words.) The next 'Träume' is *forte*, and now you sing with emotion, and with an expression of joy until you reach 'dass sie wachsen, dass sie blühen, träumend spenden ihren Duft'—and then more and more *diminuendo* and *morendo*: 'Sanft an deiner Brust verglühen und dann sinken in die Gruft'. The postlude continues *pianissimo* and fades slowly away.

MIGNONLIEDER

HUGO WOLF

Born 1860 in Windischgraetz, died in an asylum in Vienna in 1903. Wolf is unique among Lieder composers, deeply influenced by Wagner and by Wagner's speech rhythms, and yet instinct with a highly personal musical style matched to every shade of expression in the texts which he set with such passionate intensity. The Mignon songs from *Wilhelm Meister* have attracted numerous composers—Schubert himself made many settings of them—but nowhere else is there to be found so deeply sensitive an understanding of these strangely moving poems.

JOHANN WOLFGANG VON GOETHE

Born 1749 in Frankfurt-am-Main, died 1827 in Weimar. Greatest of German literary figures and man of many and diverse accomplishments, Goethe may be said to have liberated the German lyric from the classical straitjacket of the eighteenth-century *Aufklärung* and to have provided Lieder composers of the nineteenth century with an incomparable fund of intensely *singable* poetry.

Wilhelm Meister is the son of a wealthy merchant who has longed that his son will inherit the business. But from childhood Wilhelm had a passion for the theatre, and so predictably fell in love with Marianne, a beautiful actress. In his youthful enthusiasm he saw in her an angel of virtue and purity, but when he discovers that she is anything but the paragon he had imagined, his understanding father sends him on a 'business trip'. Soon he meets some out-of-work actors and—unmindful of his duties and the purpose of his trip—he joins them. The pretty and frivolous actress Philine tries unsuccessfully to arouse his passion, but—once bitten, twice shy. . . .

One day he sees the director of a circus troop maltreating a child and he frees her from her brutal master. In point of fact, he buys her from him and she accompanies him as his 'page'. When he asks her name, she replies that she is known as Mignon. Vaguely she recalls whence she came. In early childhood gypsies had stolen her from her father's castle, and she tells Wilhelm all she can remember.

I *Kennst du das Land?*

The song starts with a sadly melancholy melody which continues with a soft crescendo until the end of 'und hoch der Lorbeer steht'. Then, quite suddenly, there comes a passionate question, even before you sing 'Kennst du es wohl?' Mignon is a strange creature. She may be only twelve years old, or she may be eighteen. It is difficult to be sure, and she herself does not know. She is like a child of the wilderness and hides her passionate temper behind a gentle, childish mask. But here, so to speak, she breaks loose. 'Kennst du es wohl?' After she repeats the question, the music dies down to *pianissimo*. But then, with renewed passion: 'Dahin möcht' ich mit dir, o mein Geliebter, zieh'n'. Slowly the veil rises from her memory and she asks Wilhelm whether he knows the house where she once lived. It was so splendid, so elegant, and there was a long corridor where marble statues gazed at her. She was always a little frightened when she passed them, but now she knows that they meant well. They used to ask her: 'Was hat man dir, du armes Kind, getan?' again, the passionate cry: 'Kennst du es wohl? Dahin! dahin möcht' ich mit dir, o mein Beschützer, zieh'n'.

The third verse reminds her of the time when the gypsies stole her. They took her over a high mountain, and when she cried, they threatened her that there were dragons living in the dark cavern who would seize her, and that the waterfall tumbling down to the valley would drown her. Oh, there she would go with her master, her rescuer; for then she would know where her home was, not far from there. 'O Vater, lass uns zieh'n!', she begs. But Wilhelm does not know where her homeland is. . . .

II Heiss mich nicht reden

This sad and melancholy song has really nothing to do with Mignon's earlier life. It is simply a song which she sang during a performance. Sing it *piano* and with suppressed emotion. There is a *crescendo* at the phrase: 'Ich möchte dir mein ganzes Innre zeigen', but at once the *pianissimo* returns.

When you sing of the rising sun, the accompaniment ascends in powerful chords so that 'Der harte Fels schliesst seinen Busen auf' is a continuation of this progression. 'Ein jeder sucht im Arm des Freundes Ruh'' must be sung with emotion and with a deep longing ('all others may complain, only I myself must remain dumb . . .'). Sing with great conviction: 'und nur ein Gott vermag sie aufzuschliessen.' The word 'Gott' is the climax and must be sung with a strong *fortissimo*. You cannot, of course, make a real *fermate* on the word 'Gott', but you can sing a little slower—and then fade away at 'vermag sie aufzuschliessen'. The short postlude expresses the harsh fate which has compelled you to keep silent.

III *Nur wer die Sehnsucht kennt*

Mignon suffers much from her frustrated love and she pours out all her longing in this lovely song.

It is perhaps better known in Tchaikovsky's setting. But Wolf's noble and much more restrained treatment appeals more to me. The introduction describes the agonies of un-requited love. The last bar before the entry of the voice is like a tormented cry. And then, in a sighing *pianissimo* you sing: 'Nur wer die Sehnsucht kennt, weiss was ich leide!' Each *crescendo* in tone and emotion *you must feel*, and also the inter-lude which is, as it were, a commentary on your own deep longing. 'Es schwindelt mir'—quite softly; and then with a heartrending cry: 'Es brennt mein Eingeweide'. There are few more passionate moments in music; and your last 'Nur wer die Sehnsucht kennt' is little more than a pathetic sigh.

IV *So lasst mich scheinen*

Mignon's health is delicate. She has frightening convulsions when she is aroused to jealousy. Wilhelm sends her away to recover, but she is so unhappy far from him that she becomes increasingly ill. Children who have attached themselves to her ask her to perform for them. She wants to please them and plays an angel in a beautiful white gown with golden wings. Her song is like a premonition of her approaching end. 'So lasst mich scheinen, bis ich werde'.

Sing this song as if you are already gone from this earth. The whole song should have an unearthly quality. The *crescendi* are scarcely perceptible, and only as you sing the last phrases do you go from *piano* slowly into a strong *forte*: 'Zwar lebt' ich ohne Sorg' und Mühe, doch fühlt' ich tiefen Schmerz genung. Vor Kummer altert' ich zu frühe, macht mich auf ewig wieder jung!' The postlude comments sadly: 'Yes, but you have first to go through the dark door which will guide you to Heaven.'

LIEDER EINES FAHRENDEN GESELLEN

GUSTAV MAHLER

Born at Kalischt in Bohemia, 1860, died in Vienna, 1911.
From 1897 to 1907 he was the controversial Director of the
Vienna Court Opera. His highly individual contribution to
the late Romantic school of Lieder lies chiefly in orchestral
songs and song cycles which exploit with great subtlety the
possibilities of orchestral colour and the equally subtle range
of the human voice.

   Lieder eines Fahrenden Gesellen (*Songs of a Wayfarer*) was his
second song cycle, composed in 1883 to his own text, with
orchestral accompaniment.

I Wenn mein Schatz Hochzeit macht

Mahler made it rather easy for the singer by explaining very precisely the correct interpretation. For instance, he says at the beginning that particular emphasis must be given to the continuous change of tempo. The song starts with the gay sounds of music which will enliven the wedding party. But at once it changes to the loneliness of the wayfarer. 'Wenn mein Schatz Hochzeit macht, hab' ich meinen traurigen Tag!'— this in a *very slow* tempo. But you are always interrupted by the gay wedding music. It is in your head and in your heart that you hear it; it pursues you constantly when you retreat into your dark and lonely room. There you are alone and can weep your bitter tears. The word 'Wein'!' must be sung very distinctly and with a big *ritardando*. But you want to forget this unhappiness. You stand at the window, you walk out of the room into the flowering garden. Nature cannot be sad with you. Nature wants to be generous, wants to console you with flowers and bird song—and you say in softest *pianissimo*: 'Blümlein blau! Verdorre nicht! Vöglein süss, du singst auf grüner Heide! Ach, wie ist die Welt so schön.' You force yourself to see the beauty around you, you force yourself to appear gay and carefree. So you imitate the bird song with a whistling 'Ziküth!' But the accompaniment is more honest than you: it fades into a sad-sounding *pianissimo*—and you admit to yourself that there is no point in this self-deception. So you close your eyes and ears to beauty and tell yourself that everything is over and done with. From afar comes the sound of the wedding music, but you do not listen to it. You are alone in your room in the evening and can think only of yourself, of the agony which love has brought to you. The *crescendi* are in your *emotion*, not in the *power* of your *voice*. And slowly, slowly, your voice fades away—and with it the wedding music.

II Ging heut' morgen über's Feld

You have made up your mind to forget. You walk in the fields and your step is steady and full of vigour. The accompaniment walks with you in a steady rhythm. The first phrase, 'Ging heut' morgen über's Feld', has a slight *staccato*, but do not overdo this. It should not sound harsh or deliberate. You pass immediately into *legato*. You listen to the finch and seem to understand what the little bird is telling you. He says: 'Good morning!' to you and is so happy that he asks you: 'Wird's nicht eine schöne Welt?' and sings his lovely 'Zink, Zink!' and bursts out in sheer delight: 'Wie mir doch die Welt gefällt!'

There is a short interlude with a soaring *crescendo* and *decrescendo* which fades into a sudden *pianissimo* and gives you the opportunity to listen to the tiny voices of the bluebells which say 'Guten Morgen!' to you and playfully sing: 'Kling, kling, wird's nicht eine schöne Welt? Wie mir doch die Welt gefällt!', and end with an exultant 'Heiah!'

The accompaniment moderates from a strong *crescendo* and now you sing with the sweetest *pianissimo*: 'Und da fing im Sonnenschein gleich die Welt zu funkeln an.' Give strong (but *pianissimo*) emphasis to: 'Alles, alles, Ton und Farbe gewann.' You repeat: 'Wird's nicht eine schöne Welt?', but you sing it very slowly and hesitantly and with a great *ritardando*. Amid all this beauty you feel that you yourself should be a part of it, a part of all the jubilation. Sing with the softest *pianissimo*: 'Nun fängt auch *mein* Glück wohl an?' Hope has made your heart beat with expectation. The accompaniment expresses this hope, but quite suddenly you realize—and with you, the accompaniment—that all your yearning is in vain. 'Nein, nein, das ich mein', mir nimmer, nimmer blühen kann.' The accompaniment fades away in softest *pianissimo*.

III Ich hab' ein glühend Messer

The next song is a passionate outburst of despair. You have tried so hard to be 'reasonable' and to forget. But your agony is stronger than you. So, at last, you are honest with yourself and give way to your grief. The accompaniment starts with a strong *fortissimo*, but passes into *pianissimo* before the voice enters. 'Ich hab' ein glühend Messer, ein Messer in meiner Brust.' Sing this with bitter resentment and passion. You must repeat several times the words: 'O weh!' and you must try to give them a slightly different expression each time. Take your time at the phrase: 'Das schneid's so tief in jede Freud' und jede Lust'. Then the repetition of 'Ach, was ist das für ein böser Gast!' is again in strict tempo, and so, too, the cry: 'Nicht bei Tag, noch bei Nacht, wenn ich schlief! O weh, o weh!' The accompaniment continues to echo this cry, but grows slower and slower—and your 'O weh!' is like a sigh. What is it, that will not let you master this passion? Slowly, whispering, you tell yourself what is happening to you: 'Wenn ich in den Himmel seh', seh' ich zwei blaue Augen steh'n! Wenn ich im gelben Felde geh', seh' ich von fern das blonde Haar im Winde weh'n!' and the 'O weh!' is once more full of passion. Now sing in a strong *accelerando*: 'Wenn ich aus dem Traum auffahr' und höre klingen ihr silbern Lachen'. This is *forte*, *accelerando*, and every syllable has a strong emphasis (*'ihr silbern Lachen'*). You cannot even finish what you wanted to say. You can only cry out: 'O weh!', and then with the full power of your voice, you at last confess what is in your mind: 'Ich wollt' ich läg' auf der schwarzen Bahr', könnt' nimmer, nimmer die Augen aufmachen'. With a marked *ritardando*, you end the song, fading away into *pianissimo*.

IV *Die zwei blauen Augen*

After this wild outburst, you seem to be utterly exhausted. The blue eyes of your beloved have sent you out into a world where you are foreign to everything and everybody. To say good-bye to the one place you love was not easy for you and you ask yourself: You have gone away in the dark night over the dark heath and nobody has said good-bye to you. Your only companions were love and sorrow. The melody fades away in a whispering *morendo*. And now you sing until the end of the song, *always in soft pianissimo*: 'Auf der Strasse stand ein Lindenbaum, da hab' ich zum ersten Mal im Schlaf geruht. Unter dem Lindenbaum, der hat seine Blüten über mich geschneit, da wusst'ich nicht, wie das Leben tut, war alles, ach alles wieder gut, alles, alles! Lieb' und Leid und Welt und Traum!'

How can one ever describe what here has been expressed in this incredibly beautiful music? The song of nature is consoling, the great wisdom that everything will have an end, good or bad—*everything*. Nature takes you into her arms and sings, with the voice of a soft wind, a cradle-song and you are safe as if in the arms of your mother. All this is told to you in the wonderful music which rocks like a cradle and lulls you to sleep.

VIER LETZTE LIEDER

RICHARD STRAUSS

Born 1864 in Munich, died 1949 in Garmisch. The last of the great Romantics, his early compositions included many Lieder (more than 150 in all) before he turned his attention first to orchestral tone-poems and then to his true *métier*, opera. More than any other composer, he glorified the *soprano* voice ('A tenor', he once said in a famous aside, 'is a dreadful thing!') I was privileged to sing many times with Richard Strauss and was even called 'Strauss Sängerin', which always flattered me. I recall with special pleasure the time when I studied with him the part of the Dyer's Wife in *Die Frau ohne Schatten* at his lovely home in Garmisch. *Vier letzte Lieder* is his last composition, written in 1948, and first performed in London by Kirsten Flagstad with Wilhelm Furtwängler. Not only are these exquisite orchestral songs Strauss' farewell; it might equally be said that they represent the end of a great and noble German tradition.

Of the four songs, the first three are settings of poems by *Hermann Hesse* (1877–1962), 1946 Nobel prizewinner, and—like Strauss in his own field—the last of the Romantic lyric poets. The fourth poem—'Im Abendrot'—is by *Eichendorff* (than whom more Romantic?)

I FRÜHLING
(*Hermann Hesse*)

The first song starts with the dreamlike remembrance of other happier springs. You dreamed of them, of flowers and trees, and your voice should have the quality of a singing bird. It climbs upwards, as a lark reaches for the blue sky, and you stop with the sudden realization that the longed-for spring has really come. There it is at your feet, in glory and splendour, like a miracle. Your voice again soars upwards in utter delight. You greet spring as if it were a friend who knows you and recognizes you, and lures you away from darkness and melancholy into the light. You feel in your whole being its blissful presence. How better could you welcome it than with the songs of birds? Your voice soars, ecstatic as a chorus of larks in the spring sky.

II SEPTEMBER
(*Hermann Hesse*)

Summer has passed. It was the fulfilment of all your dreams. But now autumn has come, and the garden mourns the passing of time. The rain falls, soft and cool, upon the last flowers. Your voice sings very gently the rhythm of the falling rain-drops. Summer trembles and waits for its end. The golden leaves of the acacia begin to fall, and the accompanying music mirrors the beauty of this golden death. Summer smiles in astonishment because it knows overwhelming beauty and feels the strangeness of the dying garden. As in spring, the voice imitates bird songs, but here much more gently, and as if tired and longing for sleep. Summer stands by the rose bush, this bright bouquet of love and ecstasy, and the accompanying music tells of adventures and of fulfilment. But summer now seeks rest and slowly closes its tired eyes. The postlude is like a cradle-song, fading away into softest *pianissimo*.

III BEIM SCHLAFENGEHEN
(*Hermann Hesse*)

The prelude climbs upwards like a sigh, and your voice starts in the same mood. The day has wearied you, and you long, like a sleepy child, for rest, and the soothing darkness of night. Your hands should stop working, your brain thinking, all of your senses want only to rest. The interlude leads the soul to freedom, and liberates it from all the fetters of the day. Your soul spreads its wings and soars into space, there to live a full and manifold life. The postlude sweeps away with the soul into light and heavenly freedom.

It is strange that Strauss, in these songs, has written with such sweeping force for the voice. A coloratura may not have the strength and power which is necessary here, while a lyric-dramatic voice perhaps has not the easy flow of tone which is necessary in the first song. But Strauss never made it easy for the singer.

IV IM ABENDROT
(*Eichendorff*)

The long prelude tells of the time you and your beloved have walked together through life, and you start with the words: 'Wir sind durch Not und Freude gegangen Hand in Hand'. Now you are tired, and rest high above the silent land. The valleys already lie in shadow. Only two larks still climb dreamily into the fragrance of the evening. The accompaniment sings with the larks high above the valley, but you do not care for this song. You want to be close to your beloved, afraid that you may lose your way in the darkness. How wonderful is the silent peace in this loneliness! The sun goes down in glory, 'Wie sind wir wandermüde—ist dies—etwa—der Tod?' And here Strauss with touching effect quotes from his early tone-poem *Tod und Verklärung*. Throughout the song the accompaniment carries a beautiful melody and, in the long postlude, fades away with the distant song of the larks into a serene emptiness.

NUITS D'ÉTÉ

HECTOR BERLIOZ

Born 1803 at Côte St André, died 1869 in Paris. Greatest of
the French Romantics, Berlioz was one of the true innovators
of the nineteenth century, and an incomparable orchestrator.
This cycle was composed between 1834 and 1841 and exists
in two versions—for voice and piano, and also with
accompaniment of small orchestra.

THÉOPHILE GAUTIER

Born 1811, died 1872. Leader of the so-called 'Parnassians',
he was art and drama critic of *La Presse*, wrote poetry and
short stories and numerous works on travel and on the history
of art.

I VILLANELLE

The first song is like a lovely painting of a rural scene. The accompaniment is like light footsteps and always slightly *staccato*. It is so lovely and uncomplicated a joy to walk with your beloved to gather lilies of the valley in the woods. You pick the pearls which the morning has strewn upon the grass: 'Sous nos pieds égrenant les perles qu'on voit au matin trembler', and then without *ritardando* and very lightly and with a very distinct diction: 'Nous irons écouter les merles'. Repeating this phrase, you sing it slightly *ritardando*, but at the third repetition again in strong tempo: 'Nous irons écouter les merles siffler'. Spring has come—spring, the month made for lovers. Even the birds are singing love songs as they sit on their nests. So you want to sit down on the moss-covered bank, and talk and talk about your love. And above all, you want to hear the longed-for whisper: It is forever . . . 'Toujours'. You describe, always in the same gentle rhythm, how the animals of the forest approach you, and you both are going home now, your fingers entwined, to make a little basket in which to carry the wild strawberries of the woods.

II LE SPECTRE DE LA ROSE

There is an extended prelude. It is the music which you cannot forget, the music to which you danced at the ball. You dream: the rose which you wore is talking to you now, the rosy head is lying on your breast and whispers to you: 'Soulève ta paupière close, qu'effleure un songe virginal, je suis le spectre d'une rose que tu portais hier au bal'. The accompaniment sways in a dancing rhythm up and down. You feel in it the slightly intoxicated way in which you danced with a man who enchanted you and who gave you the rose, still trembling with the dewdrops or the silvery pearls of the fountain in the garden. With a lovely sweeping crescendo:

'Et parmi la fête étoilée tu me promenas tout le soir'. The rose is so happy that it could grace you the whole evening long. Your *forte* is strong and glowing and passes hesitantly into *rallentando*: 'O toi qui de ma mort fus cause', and then with an almost fanatical joy: 'Sans que tu puisses le chasser, toutes les nuits mon spectre rose à ton chevet viendra danser'. The short breathing spaces between the words which follow must not be exaggerated. It is as if your breath stops at the very thought of so desired a death. These breaks of music always have a *reason*. To *feel* this reason and make it your own is very important. The soul of the dying rose comes, heavy with its lovely scent, directly from Paradise. You sing this with a great sweeping power, *allargando* and *crescendo*. The rose is not sorry that it must die, because it dies on the alabaster of your breast, and the poet says that every king will envy such a fate. He says so with a kiss, but he was only allowed to tell the tale. The rose, it seems, has a better fate than he.

III SUR LES LAGUNES

This song is a sad lament. Your beloved friend, your wife, has died. The piano music sighs with you, and for a long time only expresses your grief with the same rhythm, the same notes. 'Sous la tombe elle emporte mon âme et mes amours'. You know that you never can be happy again, because she took your soul and your love with her into the grave: 'Dans le ciel, sans m'attendre, elle s'en retourna'. The angel who took her up to Heaven refused to take you too: 'Que mon sort est amer! Ah! sans amour s'en aller sur la mer!' This 'Ah!' is an outbreak of grief. It is a *sudden forte*, but do not sing it only as a *vocal forte*, it must arise from an intense emotion and should not sound harsh; then immediately to a *diminuendo*. Now, very soft: 'La blanche créature est couchée au cercueil; comme dans la nature tout me paraît en deuil!' It is not she, your wife, whom you call 'la blanche créature', it is not her soul which was always yours in her smile and in her love for you. This 'créature' is only her dead body which has nothing to do any more with herself. The whole world seems to mourn her death, and the tame dove which used to be her pet weeps and moans and feels abandoned. The accompaniment here is different from the beginning. The lament of the dove is expressed more softly and the tempo is animated. But then, with a very passionate *crescendo*, you break out again: 'Mon âme pleure et sent qu'elle est dépareillée'. And then again, through your tears: 'Que mon sort est amer! Ah! sans amour s'en aller sur la mer!' The music now grows dark and sombre. You sing with suppressed emotion: 'Sur moi la nuit immense s'étend comme un linceul, je chante ma romance que le ciel entend seul'. All nature seems like a shroud to you, and you know that your song does not reach the ears of your dead beloved. With a sudden passionate cry you tell of her beauty, of how deeply you have loved her. The accompaniment here is fiery and *forte*. Even this *forte* rises to another crescendo so that your last lament becomes the high point of the song: 'Je n'aimerai jamais une femme autant qu'elle!' The words 'une femme autant qu'elle' must be sung very distinctly. They are followed by a *ritardando* and *diminuendo*: 'Que mon sort est amer!' and repeat almost in tears: 'Que mon sort est amer!' After a short pause, again the wild outburst: 'Ah! sans amour s'en aller sur la mer!' Fading away with the accompaniment: 'S'en aller sur la mer!' and then very *pianissimo* 'Ah! *Ah!*' The sound of his lament vanishes as if the bereaved man were disappearing over the horizon.

IV L'ABSENCE

The next song is also a lament. But it speaks of an absent beloved, one who *may*, or *will* return. The first bar is like a trumpet-call. Sing *forte*: 'Reviens, reviens'. The pause on the last word is long, and full of emotion—and then *piano*: 'Ma bien aimée!' *Pianissimo*: 'Comme une fleur loin du soleil', and the next phrase has a soft *crescendo*: 'La fleur de ma vie est fermée loin de ton sourire vermeil!' The accompaniment moves with the voice and has the same climax on the word 'loin'. The distance between these two hearts is great and cruel, the distance between the kisses unbearable. This must be sung in an animated tempo, and then very passionately and with a sweeping *crescendo*: 'O, sort amer! O dure absence! O grands désirs inapaisés!' The repetition of the lament sounds as at the beginning. Observe the long pauses between the

phrases. Then *crescendo* and *ritardando poco a poco*: 'D'ici là-bas
que de campagnes, que de villes et de hameaux! Que de vallons
et de montagnes, à lasser le pied des chevaux.' These last
words, 'à lasser le pied des chevaux', are very *forte* and distinct.
The distance between you and your beloved seems to be infinite
and you almost cease to hope that she will hear you and come
back to you. Therefore, the last repetition of your lament:
'Reviens, reviens, ma bien aimée!', is in the softest *pianissimo*.
Only when you sing: 'La fleur de ma vie est fermée loin de
ton sourire vermeil' do you rise to an emotional *crescendo*; and
then *decrescendo* again till your voice dies away, and with
you the accompaniment.

V AU CIMETIÈRE

The whole mood of this song is mysterious and uncanny.
It is evening. The sun goes down and the cemetery lies in deep
shadow. There is a white tomb on which the shadow of a yew
tree floats with a melancholy sound. This sound comes from
the song of a dove which is sad and alone and sings her plain-
tive song as the last rays of the setting sun fall upon her.

Throughout this whole part of the song the accompaniment
moves in the same *pianissimo* and quite without expression.
The dove's song is tender, and at the same time inexpressibly
sad, and as you listen to it, you, too, become desolate. Here
there is a *crescendo*, so that 'Que vous fait mal' is the high
point, and each syllable must be very distinct. You would
like to hear this strange song forever. It sounds to you as if an
angel from Heaven had fallen in love and was sadly sighing.
There is a legend that a soul, awakened, is weeping beneath
the earth—its tears are the song of the dove. It tells how
terrible it is to be forgotten and coos softly with the voice of
a dove. The accompaniment here sighs too, as it imitates the
sound of the lost soul, with marked *sforzato*. But then for a
moment it seems to recall a moment of perfect memory. The
music, which sounded more gay and earthly than before,
reverts once more to the subdued sighing of the dove. You see
a shadow, a form like an angel, pass you in a trembling ray of
light, and you repeat: 'Tu passes, passes, dans un rayon
tremblant'. The flowers of the night close and their sweet

fragrance seems to be all around you—and the nebulous form
of a ghost stretches its arms out to you and murmurs: 'Tu
reviendras!' All this is very *pianissimo* and the last 'Tu reviendras!' is like a faint echo. But now you swear to yourself that
you never will return to the grave when evening comes in its
dark mantle; and you listen to the song of the dove in the yew
tree. *Ritardando* and the faintest *diminuendo* possible, so that the
last words fade away and the accompaniment is scarcely audible.

VI L'ÎLE INCONNUE

But now, what a blessing! The last song is full of gaiety.
It starts with a lively prelude and 'Allegro spirituoso' is already
a lovely promise. A young man seeks to lure his girl away with
him. He may even have a boat, a small one. But his fantasy is
boundless and he tells her of his ship which is full of miraculous things. The boat is ready to carry her wherever she wants
to go. The accompaniment sways and dances with the poem.
The wind is favourable and the sails are set. The wind blows,
the sails fill in the welcoming wind. The boy describes the
boat with glowing pride: 'L'aviron est d'ivoire, le pavillon
de moire, le gouvernail d'or fin'. And much more than that!
For ballast he has an orange, for his sail the wings of an
angel, and the foam is a seraph. The accompaniment follows
his laughing words and swings with him into the free air and
sweeps on to his daring question: 'Where would you like to
go, my young beauty? The wind is so favourable, the sails
are all set'. And since she does not reply, he continues with
a splendidly grandiloquent gesture: 'Est-ce dans la Baltique?
Dans la mer Pacifique? Dans l'île de Java?' There is no limit
to his fantasy! So he promises her the whole world, but she
only wants to visit the island where one is always faithful and
loves forever. That makes him very embarrassed. The accompaniment hesitates—and laughs at him with some staccato
chords. But he recovers quickly and answers her truthfully:
'Cette rive, ma chère, on ne la connaît guère aux pays des
amours'. But he has not given up hope. He continues his song,
but now very subdued, very *pianissimo* and *rallentando*: 'Où
voulez-vous aller? La brise va souffler'. These last phrases are
long drawn-out. The accompaniment fades away—and does
not wait for her answer.

CHANSONS MADÉCASSES

MAURICE RAVEL

Born 1875 at Ciboure, near St Jean de Luz, died 1937, in Paris. One of the first musical Impressionists, his work—especially his songs and piano music—is marked by exquisite taste and by a highly individual sense of musical colour and sonority. These songs were composed during the years 1925–26 and were originally scored for flute, cello and piano accompaniment.

EVARISTE (DÉSIRÉ DES FORGES) PARNY

Born 1753, died 1814. The poems of this cycle are translations of native folk-songs from Madagascar.

Deep in the virgin forest, at the foot of giant mountains and hidden by tall ferns, lies the village where the natives live. They have their own rules and their own ethics but I am sure that they suffer and rejoice just as we do. And there, in this village lies the hut of the youth about whom I want to tell you.

The first song tells of the secret meeting of two lovers; it is the beautiful Nahandove for whom the young man is waiting. She seems to come often to his hut which he has built from bamboo stems and covered with palm leaves. He lets the night know that the night birds have started their song, that the moon is shining, and the dew falls on his burning forehead. 'This is the hour', he says. 'Who could keep you from coming?' The piano music is very hesitant and gives full freedom to the voice. The youth has prepared a beautiful bed that shall be worthy of Nahandove's loveliness. 'Le lit de feuilles est préparé; je l'ai parsemé de fleurs et d'herbes odoriférantes. Il est digne de tes charmes, Nahandove, oh, belle Nahandove!' Suddenly the piano music starts in a faster tempo, as if in imitation of Nahandove's quick footsteps. 'Elle vient, j'ai reconnu la respiration precipitée que donne une marche rapide. J'entends le froissement de la pagne qui l'enveloppe.' The accompaniment sweeps upwards in a broad *crescendo*, as he cries out in delight: 'It is she! It is she! It is Nahandove, la belle Nahandove!' And at this last word one imagines a passionate embrace. Then the music dies down to the softest *pianissimo*. 'Oh, reprends haleine, ma jeune amie! Repose-toi sur mes genoux!' And he delights in her enchanting glances and feels under his caressing hands her beating heart. All this is of course very *pianissimo*. The music describes the ecstasy of their supreme moment. 'Tes baisers penètrent jusqu' a l'âme, tes caresses brûlent tous mes sens. Arrête, ou je vais mourir! Meurt' on de volupté, Nahandove, o belle Nahandove?'

After a violent *crescendo* and *accelerando*, the music dies down into a beautiful melody, like a cradle-song, and he tells her tenderly that now her breathing is quiet again, that her beautiful eyes, full of tears, are closed, and that her passion is spent and she has become languid. 'Jamais tu ne fus si belle, Nahandove, o belle Nahandove!'

Now she leaves him, and he is alone with his desire. He must wait until evening comes. Then she will be back again—'will you, Nahandove, belle Nahandove?'

The music fades into *pianissimo* and we imagine the youth falling asleep, dreaming of that passionate moment, and smiling at the remembrance of it.

II AOUA!

The men of the island have a meeting. They sit around the fire smoking their pipes filled with sweet-smelling, sun-dried tobacco leaves and listening to their leader. He is the richest man on the island, with several wives and the best hut, the best goats and sheep. He has the respect of the villagers. They know that he guides them rightly and justly. One of his wives may be the beautiful Nahandove. She would have time to-night to return to her lover. The men have more important business on their minds tonight. They want to listen to their chief.

The first cry 'Aoua!' has to be uttered as strongly as possible. The piano cries out with it, and we can see the tall man standing there in the midst of his followers, with the reflection of the fire on his dark face. He warns them with his piercing cry: 'Do not trust the white men, you people of this island!' The music turns to a soft *pianissimo*. It sounds like a song of mourning for the dead; and the leader tells them the old story they have heard before and want to hear again.

In the days of their ancestors the white men descended on this island. They were told: 'Here is the soil which your women may cultivate. Be good, be just, be our friends!' Throughout this speech the music continues like a threnody. The white people promised—but they went back on their promise. A great fortress was built—'le tonerre fut renfermé dans des bouches d'airain'. Their priests wanted to give them a God whom they did not know. At last they talked about disobedience and wished to make them their slaves (here the accompaniment is *accelerando* and *crescendo*); and then they threatened them with death. The battle was long and bitter, but in spite of the hail of fire 'qui écrasait des armées entières, ils furent tous exterminés'. The piano music cries out in ecstasy with the men, 'Aoua, Aoua!' and then savagely: 'Méfiez-vous des blancs!'

The music continues *accelerando* and with great force. It must sound as if quick but heavy footsteps are accompanying the words. 'We have seen your tyrants, more ruthless and more numerous. They built their great houses in our villages, but Heaven has fought on our side. It made the rains fall on them, the hurricanes and the fearful winds.' And now, *molto retardando*: 'They exist no more, and we are alive, alive and free.' But all the men bow their heads as if in fear, and they all say very softly, so that none may hear them: 'Méfiez-vous des blancs!' The piano music ends in a funeral dirge.

III IL EST DOUX

The prelude is full of languid sighs and they are sighs of contentment and lazy enjoyment. There is nothing to be excited about. . . .

The man who had spoken to his followers and had aroused their passionate hatred of the white people now rests comfortably on his bank of leaves in front of his hut. His wives have arranged this bed for him, their master, and have taken care that he is content with their efforts. He is—and they are happy with him. He says with lazy satisfaction: 'Il est doux de se coucher durant la chaleur sous un arbre touffu', and he waits until the evening wind will bring some refreshment. Softly he calls to his wives—one of whom may be Nahandove. The accompanying music is scarcely audible, and leaves the singing voice to its own devices. The man wants to hear the chatter of his wives which seems to him like music. He wants to hear the old song, the song which tells of the young girl who is busy making a mat or preparing the rice for cooking, while chasing away the greedy birds. The music imitates the fluttering of wings with a long drawn-out tremolo. The man says slowly and contentedly: 'Le chant plaît à mon âme, la danse est pour moi prèsque si douce qu'un baiser'. Here the accompaniment dies away in softest *pianissimo*. The singer's voice is left quite free to express itself. A lazy *ritardando* accompanies the voice. But now the music, always *pianissimo*, takes on a slight *accelerando*. 'Your steps are slow and they seem to imitate the pleasure and the abandon of voluptuous love'.

A pause.

You are quiet as the music continues in extended bars.

The man sits up and says: 'The evening wind is coming, the moon is rising above the mountain trees'.

A pause.

Then, with an almost expressionless voice, as if accustomed to give orders: 'Come, women, and prepare the evening meal!'

HISTOIRES NATURELLES

MAURICE RAVEL

This cycle was composed in 1906.

JULES RENARD

Born 1864, died 1910. Author of realistic novels, plays and poetry, he was the founder of the literary journal *Mercure de France*.

These songs are really duets with the piano. One cannot talk about an *accompaniment*, because the piano here illustrates the actions of the peacock so vividly that it really sings and talks with the singing voice.

The prelude shows already—without words—how the peacock struts around, very majestic and very self-important. And you sing with a very serious expression: 'Il va sûrement se marier aujourd'hui'. The piano continues to strut proudly, and you sing *parlando* and rather subdued: 'Ce devait être pour hier'. The peacock is dressed for the gala occasion. He waits only for his fiancée. And then, with a very dry tone: 'Elle n'est pas venue—elle ne peut tarder'. Vaingloriously he walks around with the bearing of an Indian prince 'et porte sur lui les riches présents d'usage'. The piano is as proud as the peacock and at the word 'glorieux', the music sweeps upwards and then struts around in a splendour of tone. Here Ravel directs that the phrases which follow are to be sung with great expression and proud emotion: 'L'amour avive l'éclat de ses couleurs et son aigrette tremble comme une lyre'. The music, which had taken on a shimmering effect when describing his appearance, dies down to *pianissimo*—and you sing *parlando* and with a dry voice: 'La fiancée n'arrive pas'.

The peacock ascends the roof and looks towards the sun. The piano prepares for his harsh cry: 'Léon! Léon!' Sing these two words as *fortissimo* as possible and as lacking in beauty as possible. The piano shrieks with him in the same tempo and also *fortissimo*.

Then comes a short pause, and you sing *parlando*: 'C'est ainsi qu'il appelle sa fiancée'. Pause. Do not enter too early with 'Il ne voit rien venir et personne ne répond'. The piano plays very softly the same rhythm with which it describes his strutting walk. The chickens in the yard do not even raise their heads. They are tired of admiring him. You must sing this section with a lazy, expressionless tone. The peacock comes down to the yard again—and the music descends with him step by step. He is utterly convinced of his beauty. These phrases have a *crescendo* and *decrescendo* and must be sung *with emotion*.

Then you sing very seriously: 'Son mariage sera pour demain'. The music after this statement is soft and it laughs quietly behind the peacock's beautiful back: 'Et, ne sachant que faire du reste de la journée, il se dirige vers le perron'. He climbs up, marching as if going to a temple, with pompous, official steps. The piano goes with him, but hesitates now, as if considering what he should do. Then it sweeps up and down in a joyous *glissando*: 'Il relève sa robe à queue toute lourde des yeux qui n'ont pu se détacher d'elle.' Then, in a majestic tempo: 'Il répète encore une fois la cérémonie'. Sing here with a very haughty expression. But the piano knows that again tomorrow the poor peacock will wait in vain for his fiancée—and closes with two short, *pianissimo* notes.

II LE GRILLON

This is the hour when the little insects who have worked like slaves come back from their daily labours, and with great concern repair the disorder in their home. The piano repeats the same lazy tune, and ends with a *pianissimo* and some whispering chords. 'D'abord il ratisse ses étroites allées de sable'. The piano imitates the scraping of the tiny broom with two *ppp* chords. 'Il fait du bran de scie qu'il écarte au seuil de sa retraite'. Again two *ppp* chords on the piano. The cricket polishes the roots of the high grass which has worried him; and the piano sings *ppp* the same tiny chords. Now comes a pause—and you sing rather breathlessly: 'Il se repose'. A *long* pause after that, and there is the sound of heavy breathing. Then: 'Puis il remonte sa miniscule montre'. And the music imitates the winding of the clock with a very, very faint tone. Then, *quite freely* (there is no accompaniment): 'A-t-il fini? Est-elle cassée?' (this with a worried expression). And the cricket rests again. Then he enters his home and closes the door. For a long time he turns the tiny key in the miniature lock, while the piano tries to help him. He listens—pause—no reason for alarm! But he is not quite sure. 'Et comme par une chainette dont la poulie grince, il descend jusqu'au fond de la terre'. The piano listens with the cricket, but *pppp*. Not a sound. A very long pause. Then sing very *legato* and *pianissimo*: 'Dans la campagne muette les peupliers se dressent comme des doigts en l'air et désignent la lune'. This must be sung very slowly, and you must see in your imagination the poplars looking up at the moon in the stillness of the night.

III LE CYGNE

The piano music throughout the song is soft and very *legato*.You must create the illusion of seeing the noble swan gliding through the water of the little lake like a white sleigh from cloud to cloud. He seeks only to catch the trembling cloud which he sees arising from the water, moving, and losing itself again in the water. There is one in particular which he desires. He aims his beak—and suddenly bending his snow-white neck, he dives into the water. Before you sing 'Il plonge', there is a *crescendo* which on the word 'plonge' has a *subito pianissimo*. The accompaniment imitates the rippling water which the swan has stirred. 'Puis, tel un bras de femme sort d'une manche, il le retire'. The music stops. Pause. He watches. 'Il n'a rien'. Pause. 'Les nuages éffarouchés ont disparu'. A *long* pause. The accompaniment which starts after the pause is slower than at the beginning of the song. The swan, not wishing to be deceived, watches the clouds coming back and deep down where the waves cease to lap, there is a cloud which forms itself into a shadow. Slowly the music returns to the quicker tempo of the beginning. Softly the swan swims nearer in his shimmering cushion of feathers, and approaches the cloud. He exhausts himself (sing this *with emotion*!), always grasping in vain for an illusion—and perhaps he will die, a victim of this mirage, without having caught one single cloud. Pause. Now sing *parlando*, really *almost speaking* in a very dry tone: 'But what do I say? Each time when he dives he stirs with his beak the nourishing mud and brings back a worm. He is growing as fat as a goose.' The piano talks with you in little *staccato* chords.

IV LE MARTIN-PÊCHEUR

The fish would not bite tonight, but I recall a rare experience. I had my line set when a kingfisher came to rest on it. There is no more brilliant bird. He looked like a big blue flower on a long stem. The rod bent under his weight.

The music throughout is mysterious. There are two chords after the slow and soft preliminary accompaniment. The first chord (two notes) is urgent and the second *rallentando*, with a short *crescendo* which end in a *subito pianissimo*.

I scarcely dared to breathe, for I was proud to think that a kingfisher had mistaken me for a tree. And I am sure that he did not fly away out of fear, but because he thought that he was rested and now flew from one branch to the next. The tempo here is slow, the music tender and always *pianissimo*.

V LA PINTADE

This is the hunchback of my yard. She does not think of pleasing anybody because of her hump. The chickens do not speak to her. The short prelude is very rapid and seems to imitate the cackling of the guinea-hen. Rudely she prepares to torment the chickens. The piano music describes how she slowly approaches them, and then quite suddenly with her head down, her body stooping, and moving swiftly on her thin legs, she strikes with her hard beak right into the centre of the red comb of a turkey hen. This is anticipated by the accompaniment—and the movement of the cruel beak is a sharp *glissando*.

This 'snob' tantalizes her. Sing very freely here. Pause. She is furious from morning till night, her head blue with rage. She fights without reason, perhaps because she imagines that someone is always making fun of her shape, her bald head and her drooping tail. The piano music here is *rallentando*, and then again suddenly accelerates. 'Et elle ne cesse de jeter un cri discordant qui perce l'air comme une pointe'. Then slow and expressive. Sometimes she leaves the yard and disappears. She allows the kindly chickens a little respite. Now the accompaniment starts *pianissimo* in a very rapid tempo, and with a big *crescendo*: 'Mais elle revient plus turbulente et plus criarde'.

The *crescendo* rises to *fortissimo*. Crazily, she throws herself to the ground. The *fortissimo* continues, but subsides into staccato chords as you sing, very dryly: 'What is the matter with her?' And then you realize, smilingly: 'The sly thing has done something absurd. She has laid an egg in the field.' Pause. 'Perhaps I will search for it if it amuses me.'

With a *glissando* the music imitates again, as at the beginning, the screeching bird which is now rolling in the sand like a crazy hunchback.

SHÉHÉRAZADE

MAURICE RAVEL

Shéhérazade was composed in 1896, with orchestral accompaniment.

TRISTAN KLINGSOR

The delectably 'Wagnerian' *nom-de-plume* of Léon Leclere, writer, painter and musician, born 1874, died 1966. This is not the *Shéhérazade* of Rimsky-Korsakov or the Thousand and One Nights, but is used simply as a derivative title meaning 'Story-telling'.

N

The accompaniment starts very *pianissimo* and very slowly, with a mysterious trembling; and your voice must be soft and dreamy as a sigh: 'Asie!' Three times 'Asie!' and in a steady *crescendo*. After these cries of longing the music remains *forte*, and then with a lovely *decrescendo* it becomes a little more animated. Now return to the first slow tempo when you sing: 'Vieux pays merveilleux des contes des nourrices', where the fantasy sleeps like an empress in a forest filled with wonders. After this the piano plays a slow melody which expresses— more than words can do—the longing to see Asia. You sing again with a sigh, 'Asie!', and be sure that your tone fits exactly the sound of the piano music. Continue in the same way: 'Je voudrais m'en aller avec la goëlette qui se berce ce soir dans le port, mysterieuse et solitaire'. The accompaniment has continued the same languishing melody and starts now to broaden with your words: 'which at last opened its violet sails like a tremendous night bird in the golden sky'. This golden sky has awakened your desire to see the wide world. You still sing *pianissimo*, but much quicker and almost breathlessly, melting into the *glissando* of the piano music: 'Je voudrais m'en aller vers des îles des fleurs'. Here the piano has another *glissando*: 'listening to the song of the wayward sea with its old bewitching rhythm'.

The 'wayward sea' is set to music which sways up and down like a wave. Your desire is great and urgent. The music is now *allegretto* and you slip into it, so to speak: 'Je voudrais voir Damas et les villes de Perse', with the slim minarets rising into the sky. Imagine now that you have to change your expression with *each description* of the desired image of your heart. For instance, you sing softly and serenely: 'Je voudrais voir de beaux turbans de soie sur des visages noirs', but then, with a strong *crescendo* and *forte*: 'aux dents claires'. You visualize the strangeness of these dark faces with their gleaming white teeth. The *forte* moderates into *piano*, but it is suppressed *pianissimo*, in which you say: 'Je voudrais voir des yeux sombres d'amour et des prunelles brillantes de joie en des peaux jaunes comme des oranges'. It is not only that you desire to *see* these people of a strange world. It is a desire to be *among* them, to see them as they are, happy or unhappy—simply *to meet them.*

Now, very softly and serenely: 'I would like to see gowns of velvet, and gowns with long fringes'. The music descends very slowly and *ppp.* Now with a serious expression, imitating the old men you want to see: 'I would like to see pipes between the lips framed by a white beard'.

Now change your expression and imitate the sly merchants whom you want to see: 'Je voudrais voir d'âpres marchands aux regards louches'. And again you must change constantly your expression to match the words: 'Et des Cadis, et des Vizirs', who have the power over life and death at a snap of the fingers. *Crescendo*: 'I would like to see Persia and India and China'. This last is on the wings of a tremendous *glissando.* Then, quite suddenly, you return to a *pianissimo* and very *staccato* accompaniment. 'The fat Mandarins under their umbrellas'—change the expression: 'Et les princesses aux mains fines'—change again: 'and the scholars who discuss among themselves poetry and beauty'.

Ah, what more can you wish to see?

The accompaniment hesitates, as if you are reflecting. Then you decide: 'I would like to be a long time in the enchanted palace and, like a traveller, contemplate the paintings': 'Des paysages peints sur les étoffes en des cadres de sapin'. The piano music hesitates as if to say: But that is not all you want to see? After a *ppp* chord and a pause, the accompaniment starts again and you know now what is still missing in your picture: 'I would like to see smiling murderers and the executioner who cuts off the head of an innocent man with his curved oriental sword'. Breathless and quicker in tempo, always *crescendo*: 'Je voudrais voir des pauvres et des reines, je voudrais voir des roses et du sang', and now, *fortissimo*: 'Je voudrais mourir d'amour ou bien de haine'. The piano music sweeps up to a strong *fortissimo* like a stormy sea until it subsides into a slow *pianissimo* again and ceases to be music at all—but simply two notes.

Very slowly now: 'And then, you come back later to tell of your adventures to those who love dreams'. And like Sinbad, raising your cup of old Arab porcelain to your lips from time to time, you interrupt your story artfully.

II LA FLÛTE ENCHANTÉE

Throughout the song there sounds the soft melody of the flute from outside the house where the girl's master has fallen asleep. The girl looks at him with scorn. He looks so absurd with his round silken cap, and his long yellow nose buried in his white beard. She listens to what the flute has to say.

The flute, which her young lover is playing, calls her with its enchanting music. And with a joyful cry, she realizes that she can now answer his call, because her master is asleep, he who always wants her to sit demurely at his side, listening to his lectures.

The music rejoices with her and accompanies her happy words: 'But I am awake, and when I come closer to the window, I hear distinctly the melody of the flute, changing from sadness to joy'. And when she draws nearer to the window, it seems to her that every note caresses her cheek like a mysterious kiss.

But she does not run down. It is too dangerous. Her master might suddenly wake and miss her. And oh! how he will chide her! So she just stands at the window and listens—and the flute speaks so beautifully to her that she forgets reality and belongs with all her being to her young lover.

III L'INDIFFÉRENT

The prelude tells you how the beautiful stranger approaches your doorstep. The music is languid and very expressive, and has only one very slight *crescendo* in the sixth bar, passing immediately to the softest *pianissimo*. You stand there and look at this lovely youth and at last find words to greet him: 'Tes yeux sont doux comme ceux d'une fille, jeune étranger'. You cannot restrain yourself. You have to tell him that the curve of his beautiful face, which has a shadow like velvet, is even more seductive in its delicate contour. The music continues to flatter the stranger. You say, captivated by his charm: 'Ta lèvre chante sur le pas de ma porte une langue inconnue et charmante', and you add in a trembling voice: 'As if it were deceptive music'.

You pause. The music stops, as if it were short of breath. And you say with all the tenderness and emotion you possess: 'Entre!' This 'Entre!' must be sung like a caress. You must feel that, if he accepts your invitation, he will be much more than just a dream to you. You continue: 'Et que mon vin te réconforte'. The music stops entirely. 'Mais non, tu passes'— and from your doorstep you see him walking away, greeting you with a last gesture full of grace. You stand there forlorn, looking at him as he walks away, his hips swaying gently in his feminine and languid way.

The music ends like a sigh of disappointment.

CHANSONS DE BILITIS

CLAUDE DEBUSSY

Born 1862 in St Germain-en-Laye, died 1918, in Paris. Debussy is one of the great revolutionary figures of music. His intensely personal harmonic idiom is at once the antithesis of Wagner's Romanticism and the creation of a new Impressionist sound which is the musical counterpart of the work of such contemporary French painters as Manet and Degas. The *Chansons de Bilitis* were composed in 1897.

PIERRE LOUYS

Born 1870, in Paris, and died there in 1925. His poetry has a subtle quality which owes much to the influence of classical Greece. Bilitis is the name Louys gave to a Moroccan girl. He implied that these poems are translations from the Greek original of her own verses, but that is no more than a poetic fancy.

The young girl who talks here about the flute is little more than a child. She is one of those girls who behave like a child but still understand all about the birds and the bees. She had received a flute from her much older boy friend and now, sitting on his knee, he teaches her to play this flute. The two bars of the introduction already convey the whimsical quality of the whole song. The singer sways slightly with the music and then starts, half whispering: 'Pour le jour des Hyacinthes il m'a donné une syrinx faite de roseaux bien taillés, unis avec la blanche cire qui est douce à mes lèvres comme le miel'. With an intimate sensuality the girl feels on her lips the sweetness of the rosewood. Like honey, she says . . . like honey it feels on her greedy lips. And she, sitting here on his knee, trembles a little to be so near to him. He plays so softly that she can scarcely hear the gentle music. Naturally the voice of the singer must reflect the same kind of hushed *pianissimo* which the words and the accompaniment indicate. Everything is *pianissimo*. The singer must give the illusion of this child, trembling on the knee of her much more sophisticated young lover, swaying slightly as if in embarrassment and at the same time in desire. Their lips meet on the centre of the flute. Very convenient, I must say! These old flutes were played from both ends, and as he teaches her how to do it, he also plays, rather cleverly, from the other end. (One day, at one of my master classes, when I was explaining the situation, I heard a voice from the audience saying, amid much hilarity: 'Some teacher!')

But everything lovely has an end. The girl suddenly realizes that it is late. The frogs are already singing their nightly songs. The girl walks quickly home, but cannot refrain from turning round to her young teacher and saying with a giggle: 'Ma mère ne croira jamais que je suis restée si longtemps à chercher ma ceinture perdue'.

II LA CHEVELURE

The first words, 'Il m'a dit', should be sung as if with suppressed laughter. Singers are often deceived by the apparently subdued opening bars. But you must imagine the situation. A girl is telling her very best friend (who has promised not to talk about it) what has happened to her. Oh, it was wonderful and so sinful! The memory makes her tremble with delight, and she cannot resist the temptation of repeating his words to her friend.

The phrases which follow must be sung with passionate desire. An artist is an extrovert. She must be able to forget herself entirely, to forget the fact that people who do not understand the vision of an artist might say: 'She sings that as if she had no shame'. But that is precisely how it should be sung! The man who tells the young woman of his dream says quite openly what he desires and what he dreams of. He says: 'J'avais ta chevelure autour de mon cou'. The accompaniment has to be as expressive as the voice. The chords are like heavy breathing. The thought that her long hair is wound around his neck and around his chest makes him sing a *crescendo* of feeling and of tone. Back again to a whispering *pianissimo*: 'Je les caressais et c'étaient les miens', and then he tells her that they were lying together 'pour toujours', bound together by the strands of her hair—and so leading to a passionate outburst: 'La bouche sur la bouche'. This must be sung with a great surge of power culminating in a broad *forte*. And then, as if exhausted by that memory: 'Ainsi que deux lauriers n'ont souvent qu'une racine'. This is again *pianissimo*. Now a steady *crescendo*: 'Et peu à peu, il m'a semblé, tant nos membres étaient confondus, que je devenai toi-même, ou que tu entrais en moi comme mon songe', ending with a strong *fortissimo*.

This is how he described his dream. And the girl continues— and here your voice must change. It must take on quite a different quality—a little trembling, a little shy, even a little frightened. 'Quand il eut achevé, il mit doucement ses mains sur mes épaules et il me regarda d'un regard si tendre que je baissai les yeux avec un frisson'. This last sentence is an

almost inaudible whisper. You must *feel* the shiver which runs
through you.

III LE TOMBEAU DES NAÏADES

Two men are walking down the snow-covered avenue.
The accompaniment is steady and completely without expression. Sing slowly and softly and as if you were feeling rather
lazy. It is so cold, even your beard is thick with little icicles,
and your shoes are heavy with snow and mud. But you are
young and eager for something that could turn into an adventure. The friend at your side is much older and much wiser
than you. He asks: 'Que cherches-tu?' And you, full of
excitement, see the footprints of a satyr. 'Je suis la trace du
satyre. Ses petits pas fourchus alternent comme des trous dans
un manteau blanc'. But your sophisticated friend sees only the
footprints of a goat. The satyrs are dead and the nymphs are
dead too. The accompaniment sounds leaden-footed and ill-
humoured. 'Depuis trente ans il n'a pas fait un hiver aussi
terrible', he says, as if he does not want to continue the con-
versation. But suddenly the music dies down to a soft *pianissimo*,
and he says, almost reluctantly: 'Mais restons içi, où est leur
tombeau'. And with the point of his cane he breaks a piece of
ice from the wall where once upon a time the Naiads danced
and laughed. The accompanying music seems to laugh and
dance on a wave sweeping upwards into the cold, pale winter
sky. Your friend, who always mocked your youthful dreams,
has much more imagination than you, though he would never
admit it. He raises the piece of ice towards the sky and looks
through it—and with the dancing music he sees the dancing
nymphs of other days through the mirror of the ice.

In the postlude you are surprised at your friend, and your
eyes ask him how and why he always wishes to be regarded
as a cynic. And the music ends with this question unanswered.

INDEX TO FIRST LINES AND
TITLES OF THE SONGS

AUTHOR'S NOTE

Throughout this book, I have deliberately avoided rendering German and French texts into English—deliberately, because the singer who wishes to study Lieder and Chansons must do so in the original language. The truly great songs are those in which the music perfectly complements and accompanies the speech rhythms and the vowel and consonant sounds of the text. With even the most expert and lyrical translation, the composer's art and genius must in some sense be debased.